ARCHAEOLOGICAL
DISCOVERIES

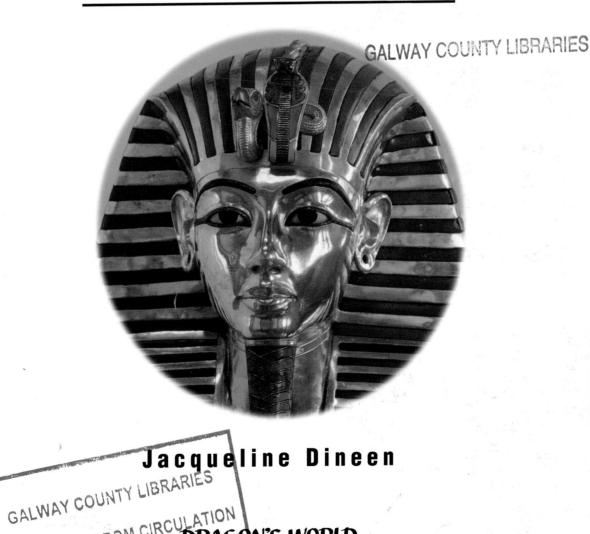

Jacqueline Dineen

DRAGON'S WORLD

CHILDREN'S BOOKS

DRAGON'S WORLD

CHILDREN'S BOOKS

Dragon's World Ltd
London House
Great Eastern Wharf
Parkgate Road
London
SW11 4NQ

First published by Dragon's World Ltd, 1997

British Library
Cataloguing in Publication Data
The catalogue record for this book is available from the British Library.

ISBN 1 85028 313 3

Editor: Diana Briscoe
Picture Researcher: Josine Meijer
Designer: Mel Raymond
Art Director: John Strange
Design Assistants: Karen Ferguson
                                 Victoria Furbisher
DTP Manager: Michael Burgess
Editorial Director: Pippa Rubinstein

Typeset by Dragon's World Ltd
in Stempel Garamond and Gill

Printed in Italy

Contents

Introduction

This book describes some of the great and most exciting archaeological discoveries that have been made since the last century when the study of archaeology began. Until then, there were many gaps in our knowledge of the past. The discoveries made by archaeologists have taught us many new things about how people lived thousands of years ago. And finds are being made all the time so we are still learning.

Few buildings are described in the book – you can find out more about those in another book in the series – *100 Greatest Manmade Wonders.* Here, we look at some of the treasures that have been found in tombs such as the pyramids of ancient Egypt, Celtic graveyards like Hallstatt in Austria, and the famous tomb of the Chinese emperor Shi Huangdi who was so afraid of death that he was buried with 600,000 life-size terracotta soldiers.

One of the more sinister burial practices was discovered by Leonard Woolley in the royal tombs at Ur. You can find out what that practice was in this book.

Archaeologists have also helped to trace the development of writing through finds such as the Egyptian Rosetta Stone and the clay tablets from the library of the Assyrian king, Assurbanipal at Nineveh. Understanding the different types of writing used long ago means that we can read ancient historical records and other documents to find out more about the organisation of early civilizations.

How did the first people evolve from their predecessors, the hominids? The discovery of bones and tools has helped us to piece together their development from 'Lucy', an apelike individual who lived in Africa over 3,000,000 years ago. We can find out about early religious practices from discoveries such as the Neanderthal grave at Shanidar in Iraq which shows that, even in 60,000 BC, our ancestors had some religious beliefs.

Excavating shipwrecks, such as the *Mary Rose* and the *Amsterdam*, tells about the design of ships in history. We can also learn from the cargo and weapons such ships were carrying when they sank. However, it is the ancients' provision for the afterlife that has given archaeologists some of their most spectacular finds.

By the time they uncovered most of the Egyptian tombs, grave robbers had broken in and stolen all the pharaohs' treasures, but there was one exception. The tomb of Tutankhamun, the boy king, was filled with magnificent gold, jewellery and every other belonging you could possibly think of. Sumptuous hoards of treasure have also been found in the New World where kings and nobles were buried with wonderfully crafted gold jewellery and death masks.

This book introduces you to these finds and many more which have helped us to build up a picture of more than 360 million years of history.

JACQUELINE DINEEN

OPPOSITE
TOP LEFT: Golden ram from Ur in Iraq
TOP RIGHT: Kim Ushin's tomb at Shilla, Korea
BOTTOM: Giant Olmec head from Mexico

BELOW: Hut made of mammoth bones from Mezhirich in the Ukraine

Archaeopteryx

Solnhofen, Germany, 160–150 mya

Archaeopteryx was the first known bird, though it was not a bird like the ones we know today. It was discovered in 1951 when a fossil skeleton was found at Solnhofen in the German state of Bavaria. No one knew what the fossil bones were, but it was thought they were from a very small dinosaur called *Compsognathus*, which lived in Europe about 140 million years ago.

However, experts who studied the skeleton again in 1973 found that the bones were from a bird which had lived about 160–150 million years ago, in the Jurassic period. It was named *Archaeopteryx*, which means 'ancient wing'.

Archaeopteryx was a strange creature which was half-reptile and half-bird. It was about the size of a crow, and it had wings and feathers. But it had other features which are not like other birds. It had teeth and it had bones in its tail. It also had claws on its wings, so it was a strange mixture.

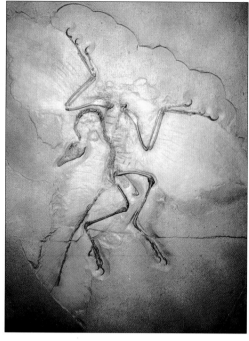

▲ Traces of feathers can be seen on this *Archaeopteryx* fossil found in Germany. This type of evidence made people realize they had found something new.

Where did *Archaeopteryx* come from? Perhaps it developed wings to help it catch insects for food. But whatever the reasons, *Archaeopteryx* was the first-known flying creature who took to the air millions of years before other birds evolved.

▼ A model of *Archaeopteryx* which was based on fossil evidence. The head is like a reptile's, but it has wings and feathers like a bird.

Iguanodon Teeth

Lewes, Sussex, 130–115 mya

Iguanodon is one of the best known of the dinosaurs because hundreds of fossil skeletons have been found in Europe and Asia. It was first discovered about 200 years ago when Mary Mantell, a doctor's wife, found some teeth on a heap of gravel near Lewes in Sussex. Mary Mantell showed the teeth to her husband, Gideon, who studied fossils as a hobby.

At this time little was known about dinosaurs and hardly any fossilized remains had been found, but Gideon Mantell realized that the teeth were unusual and very old. He showed them to various experts who thought that they probably belonged to a fish, or to a large animal, such as a rhinoceros.

Mantell was not satisfied with this. He noticed that the teeth were similar in shape to the teeth of an iguana lizard, though they were much bigger and much older. In 1825, he

▲ *Iguanodons* were unknown until Mary Mantell found the first *iguanodon* teeth near Lewes in Sussex in the early 19th century.

▼ *Iguanodons* were up to 10 metres long. They were herbivores which became prey for meat-eating species.

wrote an article in which he put forward the theory that the teeth belonged to a huge prehistoric reptile which he called *Iguanodon*, a name which means 'iguana tooth'.

As time went by, more fossilized remains of *Iguanodon* were found and people began to work out what it must have looked like. In 1842, a fossil expert called Richard Owen said that it was not a lizard at all, but a different type of reptile which no longer existed. He called these creatures 'dinosaurs', which means 'terrible reptiles'.

Iguanodons were awesome creatures. They stood 5 metres tall on their powerful hind legs. When they were hungry, they ripped leaves off trees with their tongues and cut them into pieces with bladelike teeth.

Dinosaur eggs

Egg Mountain, Montana, 75–65 mya

Since 1978, fossil hunters have uncovered hundreds of dinosaur nests and eggs near Bynum in Montana. Before the discovery of this site, which is now called Egg Mountain, people believed that dinosaurs simply laid their eggs wherever they happened to be, and then left them to hatch on their own. But the Egg Mountain finds show that some dinosaurs were careful mothers.

Some of the nests belonged to *Maiasaura*, a duck-billed dinosaur. Each nest is a hollowed-out mound of earth. When the babies hatched, she looked after them until they could fend for themselves. Other nests belonged to a smaller dinosaur, *Orodomeus*. These nests are simply flat patches of earth where between fifteen and twenty eggs had been laid. Some of the eggs had not hatched, and scientists could, by using X-rays, see the partly formed babies.

▼A model of a nest belonging to *Orodomeus*. The babies were fully developed when they hatched which was just as well since *Orodomeus* did not look after her young.

▲ An unhatched dinosaur's egg. The person's hand gives you an idea of the size of these eggs.

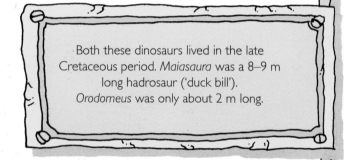

Both these dinosaurs lived in the late Cretaceous period. *Maiasaura* was a 8–9 m long hadrosaur ('duck bill'). *Orodomeus* was only about 2 m long.

Olduvai Gorge

Tanzania, c. 350,000 BC

The earliest direct ancestors of modern human beings were *Homo habilis*, or 'Handy Man'. They were descended from the earlier apelike species known as *Australopithecus*, but there were important differences. The skull of *Homo habilis* was rounded and the face looked more human. The size of the brain was larger and he could walk upright and use his hands to make tools.

The name *Homo habilis* was coined by the British archaeologist, Louis Leakey, who found the first evidence of them at the Olduvai Gorge in Tanzania. He only found fragments of bone, but he managed to identify the species, which he named 'Handy Man' because these people could make tools.

In 1972, Leakey's son, Richard, discovered the bones of a type of *Homo habilis* near Lake Turkana in Kenya. Leakey also found some simple stone tools there, the oldest examples ever found.

▲ An *Australopithecus* skull found at Olduvai Gorge. The brow is low and the face is ape-like.

▼ The Olduvai Gorge. Within the last 500,000 years a stream began to cut its way through the layers which had built up over the ancient site, exposing the evidence of bones and tools.

The Olduvai Gorge is on the site of an ancient lake. As the gorge formed over thousands of years, bones and tools were buried in the layers, making it a particularly rich site for learning about people's earliest ancestors.

'Lucy'

Hadar, Ethiopia, c. 3,400,000 BC

An important difference between humans and other animals is that humans walk upright. The earliest ape-like creatures, or hominids, which may have been the ancestors of humans, learned to do this four million years ago. Once they could walk on two legs, and their hands were freed for doing other things, they could develop in a more complex way than other animals.

The early hominids looked like the apes they were descended from. They were named australopithecines, which means 'southern apes'. The earliest and most complete example of an australopithecine skeleton was found at Hadar in Ethiopia in the 1970s. It was the skeleton of a small woman who lived about 3.5 million years ago. She was ape-like, but walked upright. This find, nicknamed 'Lucy', helped to give a clearer picture of early hominids.

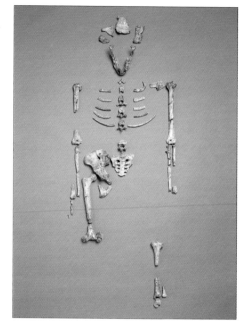

▲ The skeleton nicknamed 'Lucy' was complete enough for scientists to put together a picture of what this early hominid looked like.

▼ The first true humans, *Homo habilis*, still looked ape-like with low brows and jutting-out jaws.

Lucy had a light, fragile skeleton and a small brain in a low-browed skull. The bone above her eyes jutted out like the brow of an ape. But although she looked like an ape, she walked upright, which makes her the earliest hominid discovered so far.

Homo erectus or Java Man

Ngangdong, Java, c. 120,000 BC

Early people began to spread from Africa to other parts of the world about 1.7 million years ago. By now the early hominids had progressed to become *Homo erectus*, or 'Upright Man', who managed to adapt to many different climates and conditions.

Those who went to colder climates learned how to make clothes to keep them warm. They learned how to light a fire and make simple shelters. And, of course, they developed their weapons and tools.

Homo erectus gradually evolved into an early form of *Homo sapiens* or modern humans. Early forms of *Homo sapiens* have been found in China and in Java in Indonesia. Skulls found at Ngangdong in Java date back to 120,000 BC, and evidence of early modern people have also been found at Zhoukoudian in China.

In China, the people had organized themselves into social groups so that they did not all have to go hunting. Different people were given different tasks to carry out. This was a big step forward in the organization of communities and the start of civilization.

These people had made many advances on the earlier *Homo erectus*. They still lived by hunting and gathering, but they had more sophisticated tools, they buried their dead and they made some simple jewellery and ornaments.

▼ The jaw and teeth of Java Man, a species of *Homo erectus,* which later evolved into early forms of modern human beings.

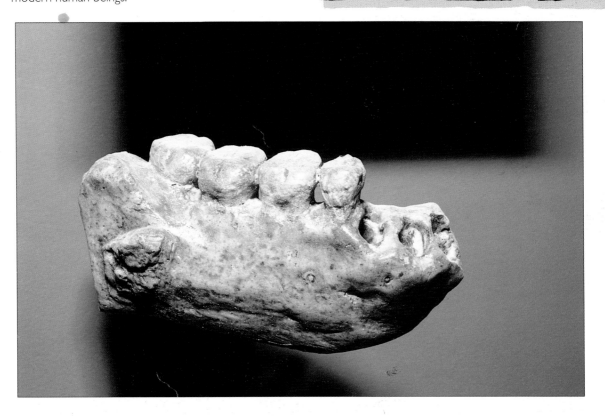

Palaeolithic Hunters

Klasies River Mouth, South Africa, c. 70,000 BC

The first ancestors of modern people developed in Africa so perhaps it is not surprising that the first truly modern humans, *Homo sapiens sapiens*, also developed there. They emerged in the southern part of Africa about 100,000 years ago, during a period known as the Middle Stone Age. These people made efficient tools and weapons by flaking the stone blades to give them sharp edges and points.

An important site for the study of these Stone Age or Palaeolithic hunters is the Klasies River Mouth in South Africa. There is evidence that people lived in caves near the river mouth between about 125,000 and 70,000 BC. They lived by collecting sea foods, such as limpets and mussels, and also hunted

the fur seals that swam in the waters. This is the first time, as far as we know, that people caught food from the sea.

The people of Klasies River Mouth also hunted land animals, such as antelope, though it seems that they avoided aggressive animals, such as the bush pig, since no bones of these animals have been found. Ashes found in the cave show that the people dried their meat as a method of storing it.

Study of this site has given a good deal of interesting information about these early and yet skilful hunters.

▼ Hunters at the Klasies River Mouth would have hunted fur seals like these, probably for their fur as much as their meat. They used spears and knives with sharp stone points fixed into wooden shafts.

This may have been the first time that people thought of things other than survival. There is evidence that they may have painted their bodies with yellow ochre and that they buried their dead.

Neanderthal Burial

Shanidar, Iraq, c. 60,000 BC

The Neanderthal people lived between 100,000 and 30,000 years ago, and they spread throughout Europe and into western Asia. They seem to have been some of the first people to have religious beliefs and to bury their dead with special rituals.

The grave of a Neanderthal man at Shanidar in the Zagros Mountains of Iraq shows that these people believed in some sort of afterlife. The man had been buried with flowers around him, and some of these were known to have healing properties. The man was also a cripple. His bones showed that he had lost his right arm as a child and that he had arthritis, a disease of the joints.

▲ The Shanidar grave was discovered in 1960. Here, the skull is being cleaned at the excavation headquarters.

▼ The entrance to the Shanidar cave. The column of dust in the picture shows where a dynamite charge had been set off to break up the rock.

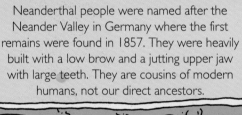

Neanderthal people were named after the Neander Valley in Germany where the first remains were found in 1857. They were heavily built with a low brow and a jutting upper jaw with large teeth. They are cousins of modern humans, not our direct ancestors.

Stone Age Burial

Sungir, Russia, c. 24,000 BC

In earlier times, when people died their friends did not know what to do with their bodies and probably simply left them where they were. Then people began burying their dead in about 80,000 BC, the beginning of what is known as the Middle Palaeolithic period.

By the Upper Palaeolithic period, which began in about 35,000 BC, burials had become more elaborate and grave goods (things buried with the dead person) were included. This suggests that people now had some religious beliefs about an afterlife.

The sites of Upper Palaeolithic burials found at Sungir, near Moscow, date back to about 24,000 BC. In one grave, the body of an old man had been buried with armlets and bracelets made of ivory. Two small boys had been buried with ornaments made of ivory and fox teeth, and weapons which included spears made from mammoth tusks. Each body was also surrounded by a row of beads made from ivory.

The painstaking work involved in making all these ornaments took thousands of hours. This is remarkable for people who lived by hunting and had to spend much of their time concentrating on survival.

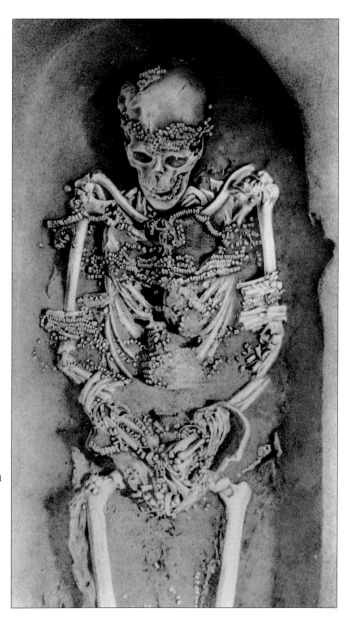

▲ This old man's body had been decked with ornaments before he was buried. Fox's teeth had been sewn on to his cap and he wore about two dozen ivory armlets and bracelets.

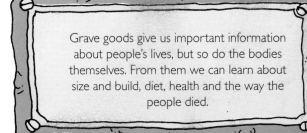

Grave goods give us important information about people's lives, but so do the bodies themselves. From them we can learn about size and build, diet, health and the way the people died.

Koonalda Cave

Southern Australia, c. 18,000 BC

Early hunters who settled in Australia between 50,000 and 60,000 years ago, needed flints to make tools and weapons. Flint occurs in limestone and ancient fingerprints found on the walls of the limestone Koonalda Cave, on the southern coast of Australia, show that this was an early flint mine.

At least 20,000 years ago, these early miners dug with their fingers into the soft limestone to take out the flints they needed. This must have been some feat. The cave was 60 m down and the miners would have worked in total darkness.

Flint could be fashioned into sharp tools for killing animals for meat, and so it became a sought after material. There were few sources of flint, and the Koonalda Cave was the only reliable source that the hunters could use.

▲ Hunters made flint axes like this one from flints dug out of the Koonalda Cave. They made them by chipping one piece of flint with another to shave off flakes and sharpen the edges.

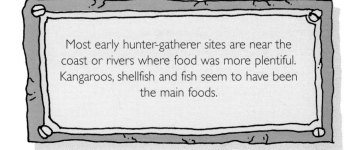

Most early hunter-gatherer sites are near the coast or rivers where food was more plentiful. Kangaroos, shellfish and fish seem to have been the main foods.

▼ The Aboriginal people came to Australia about 60,000 years ago and spread widely very quickly. Sites dating from 50,000 to 25,000 BC are marked with circles; those from 25,000 to 10,000 BC with triangles. Koonalda Cave is in the centre at the bottom.

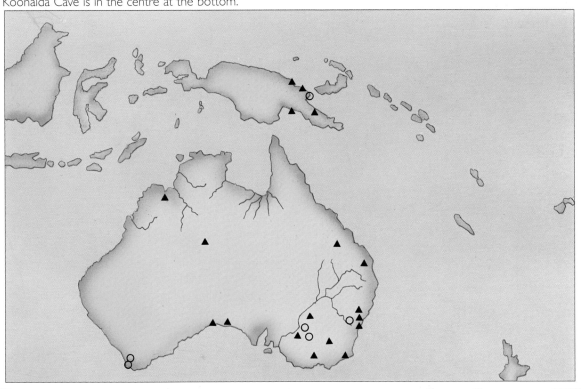

Cro-Magnon Cave

Dordogne, France, c. 20,000 BC

About 35,000 years ago, a new type of human began to emerge. This was *Homo sapiens sapiens*, who is also known as Cro-Magnon Man, because their remains were first found in the Cro-Magnon cave in France. *Homo sapiens sapiens* is the first true ancestor of modern humans. The Cro-Magnons were far more sophisticated than earlier peoples, and made many discoveries which helped humans to develop more quickly.

Early people had been making simple tools for thousands of years. They made crude hand axes and clubs by chipping away bits of stone or bone to get the shape they wanted. *Homo sapiens sapiens'* tool-making techniques were far more sophisticated than earlier methods. They used a wooden punch to give their tools sharp points. Bone or ivory was made into fish-hooks, spearheads, and harpoon heads. A key invention was the burin, a sharply pointed tool for carving or shaping wood, bone or flint.

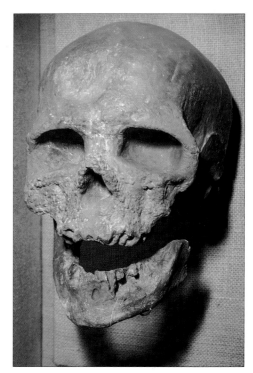

▲ This skull shows that Cro-Magnon Man had a higher brow and smaller jaw than the earlier ape-like hominids.

▼ Cro-Magnon people were cave dwellers. The Dordogne region of France, where their remains were first found, is rich in prehistoric remains.

By about 20,000 years ago, the last Ice Age had reached its coldest point and the people had a struggle to survive. They invented bows and arrows so that they could hunt woolly mammoth and other animals. They learned how to make clothes and tents from skins.

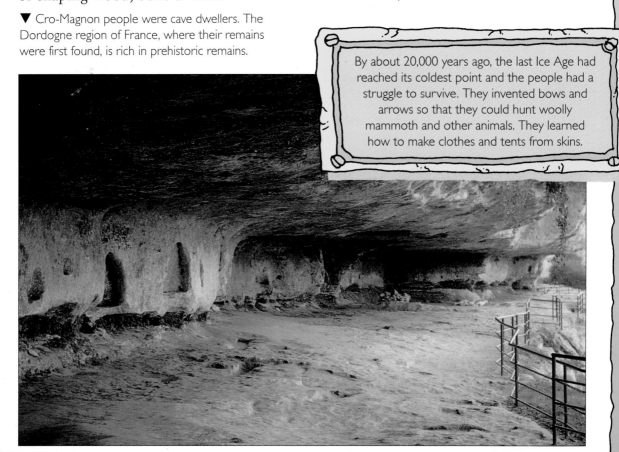

Venus of Willendorf

Austria, c. 20,000 BC

By about 30,000 years ago, people could spare the time from the endless task of hunting for food to express themselves in art. They painted on the walls of caves and also produced simple sculptures. Many of these were figures of women which do not look very flattering to us today, though they are known to archaeologists as Venuses. The figures were almost all small and fat and were carved from stone, bone or ivory.

One of the earliest and most famous is the Venus of Willendorf, which was found in Austria. It is a small statue of a woman with huge breasts and thighs, but no real facial features. She does not look very attractive to Western eyes, although to other cultures today, she might. So, why did the Stone Age artists carve women in such a way?

One theory is that these statues represented goddesses of fertility, and their ample figures suggested the richness of the earth. But perhaps women really did look a bit like that in those days. These statues were carved during the last Ice Age when the winters were so cold that people could not survive unless they developed a large supply of fat in their bodies during the summer. But no one really knows what the truth behind these strange statues is.

▲ The Venus of Willendorf was carved from stone. She has hair, but no facial features. She may have been used in rituals to do with finding food, or giving thanks for a successful hunt.

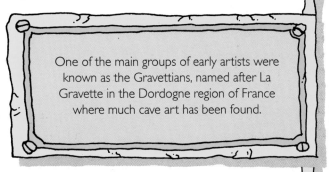

One of the main groups of early artists were known as the Gravettians, named after La Gravette in the Dordogne region of France where much cave art has been found.

Mammoth Hut

Mezhirich, Ukraine, c. 15,000 BC

The last Ice Age reached its peak about 20,000 years ago, and survival was hard for the hunter-gatherers who lived then. They had to develop new tools and hunting techniques. The landscape changed as well as the climate. Woodlands disappeared and were replaced by open grasslands, so wood was scarce. The hunter-gatherers learned to make the things they needed from materials such as bone and antler.

Shelter was important for survival. There was no wood to build shelters from, so what could the people use? The remains of a hut found at Mezhirich in the Ukraine gives us an answer. The woolly mammoth was one of the Ice Age animals which provided the people with food, skins and bones. And the massive bones could be used to build shelters. The shelter at Mezhirich was made from 385 mammoth bones, packed together in a circular shape.

The ground inside the shelter had been hollowed out to form a pit. Charcoal and ash found there suggest that there may have been a hearth for cooking, but two hearths were also found outside the hut. In one, bones had been propped up, perhaps to form a structure for cooking on.

The remains of many other mammoth huts have been found in the Ukraine. Although they have long since collapsed and been buried, archaeologists can work out from the position of the bones what the huts must have looked like.

Hunter-gatherers also made shelters from skins stretched over mammoth tusks. Shelters like these could be packed up and people could take them with them when they travelled from one place to another looking for animals to hunt.

▼ The hunters built their huts by fitting large mammoth bones tightly together to keep out the cold. A pair of tusks frame the opening to the hut.

Hunter-gatherer Village

Monte Verde, Chile, c. 13,000 BC

The wooden buildings in this village in southern Chile had been preserved for thousands of years before archaeologists discovered them. The village is so well-preserved that it gives us a clear picture of the type of huts and shelters used by hunter-gatherers before the days of settled communities. The twelve rectangular huts had wooden frames covered with the hides of mastodon, a type of elephant which is now extinct.

On one side of the village was a structure containing the remains of plants that are known to contain healing properties. This may have been the place where medicines were made and given to people who were sick or had been wounded.

We do not know when these people reached Chile, but their knowledge of the area and the plants and animals there suggest that it was long before the village was built.

▼ The people who lived at Monte Verde may have looked rather like these hunters, bringing home a kill to be cooked over the open fire.

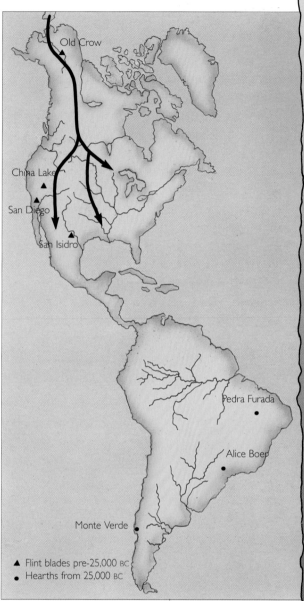

▲ Flint blades pre-25,000 BC
• Hearths from 25,000 BC

▲ It is thought that the first people came into the Americas by crossing the Baring Strait into Alaska and then spreading southwards. This happened about 40,000 years ago. Certainly there is evidence of people living in South America from about 32,000 BC onwards.

People had settled in South America thousands of years before the village at Monte Verde was built. There is evidence that people settled at Pedra Furada in Brazil as early as 32,000 BC. A rock shelter with a hearth and some tools has been found there.

Cave Art

Altamira, Santander, Spain, c. 12,000 BC

About 35,000 years ago, in Europe, the first modern humans produced the continent's first art. But why did people begin to draw and paint?

As people developed over thousands of years, their brains became larger and more efficient. They could look beyond the day-to-day business of finding food and ask themselves about the world around them. Perhaps they asked themselves who controlled everything they saw, and this led to a belief in some type of god.

We do not really know why people began to draw and paint, but it may have had something to do with their religious beliefs. Perhaps they believed that drawing the animals they hunted would bring them luck. The painted

cave at Altamira, near Santander in Spain, shows animals which are nearly life-size. There are bison, horses, boar and deer.

The cave was discovered in 1879, but people did not realize its true age until 1902. The cave is very dark so the artists must have worked by lamps fuelled with animal fat. The paintings are in different colours made from minerals.

Cave paintings are interesting because they give us evidence about animals at the time and also show how art developed from the very beginning.

▼ A bison painted on to the wall of the Altamira cave. The artists used natural minerals such as ochre to make their paints, which they often put on the walls with their hands, or with a stick or a brush made from animal hair.

Art that could be moved from place to place, such as sculpture, seems to have begun slightly earlier than wall art. Early artists also engraved animals on to small pieces of stone, bone or antler.

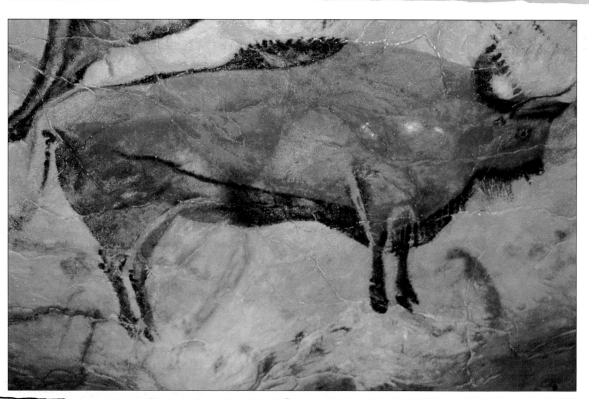

Folsom Flints

New Mexico, USA, c. 10,000 BC

One day in 1925, a cowboy called George McJunkin was riding along the edge of a gully in New Mexico when he saw something white glittering in the sun. When he looked more closely, he saw that it was a pile of bleached bones. Among the bones was a delicately shaped flint blade.

When the experts examined the finds, they identified the bones as belonging to a type of bison which had been extinct for about 10,000 years. The blade among the bones suggested that the animal had been killed by a hunter. But there had not been big game hunters in North America 10,000 years ago. Or had there?

Archaeologists were doubtful at first because no human remains had been found. Perhaps the blade had been made much later and had somehow become mixed up with the bones. But then further exploration of the site revealed

▲ One of the many flint blades found at Folsom. The delicate carving of the point shows that the Paleo-Native Americans who lived there over 10,000 years ago were skilled toolmakers.

another discovery. This time, it was the skeleton of an ancient bison with a stone spearhead embedded in its ribs. This was proof that the animal had been killed by a hunter.

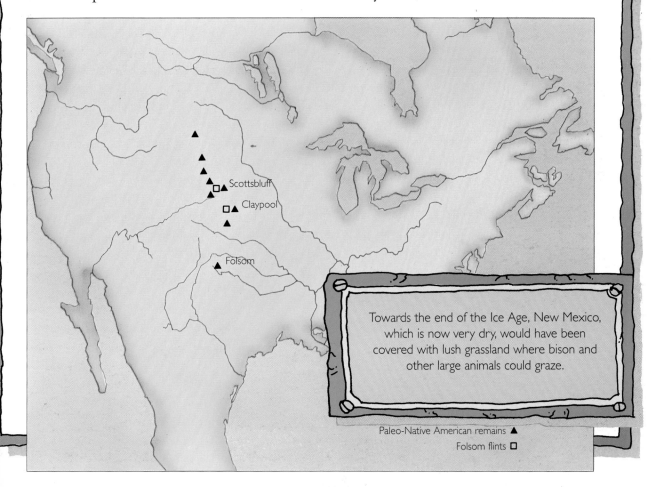

Scottsbluff

Claypool

Folsom

Towards the end of the Ice Age, New Mexico, which is now very dry, would have been covered with lush grassland where bison and other large animals could graze.

Paleo-Native American remains ▲
Folsom flints ◻

Rock Art

Sahara Desert, Algeria, c. 8500 BC

Today, the Sahara Desert in northern Africa is one of the driest places in the world. But it was not always so. At the end of the last Ice Age, about 12,000 years ago, the ice sheets which had covered Europe and Asia melted and lakes appeared in the desert.

As some of the water evaporated, rain began to fall and plants and trees began to grow. Bands of hunters and gatherers moved into the Sahara. The rock paintings they made in the caves of the Hoggar Mountains give us an idea of the lives they led.

The earliest of these paintings date back to about 8500 BC and show the range of animals that the hunters caught. They featured elephant, rhinoceros, hippopotamus, giraffe and a type of buffalo. Later paintings show that the hunters had begun to tame animals, such as giraffe and a type of cattle.

▲ Paintings such as this hunter and animals tell us about life in the Sahara before it became a desert.

About 7,000 years ago, the climate changed again and the Sahara began to dry up. The animals either died out completely or moved elsewhere. The people were forced to move as well. Some of them went to Egypt where they settled by the banks of the River Nile and became the first Egyptians.

◄ The rock paintings show that, among others, giraffe and hippopotamus once lived in the Sahara.

The Settlement at Çatal Hüyük

Turkey, c. 7000 BC

Çatal Hüyük is a large Neolithic settlement in southern Turkey. It was founded in about 7000 BC, and at its height 5,000 people lived there. The mud-brick houses were clustered together and there were no outside doors. People went in and out of the houses through openings in the roofs.

The people of Çatal Hüyük were farmers, but they managed to organize their lives efficiently and soon became prosperous. Like other early farmers, they worried about the weather and the seasons. Would their crops grow well? Would there be a successful harvest? To them, it all depended on the gods.

We know something about religious life at Çatal Hüyük from the magnificent shrines, wall paintings and religious objects found at the site. The people worshipped an Earth Goddess who was often shown as a leopard on wall paintings.

There were also at least forty shrines dedicated to a bull god, who was represented by a huge bull's head. The heads were modelled in clay, but were shaped around the skull of a bull and sometimes real bull's horns were added.

When people died, their bodies were left in the open so that the vultures could pick them clean. Then the bones were buried under houses or shrines. In houses, the bones were put under the sleeping platform.

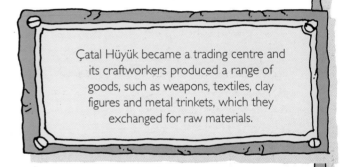

Çatal Hüyük became a trading centre and its craftworkers produced a range of goods, such as weapons, textiles, clay figures and metal trinkets, which they exchanged for raw materials.

▼ A wall painting of a bull from a shrine at Çatal Hüyük. Gods were always symbolized by a bull.

Settlement at Lepenski Vir

Former Yugoslavia, c. 6000 BC

As the ice melted after the last Ice Age, about 12,000 years ago, the sea level rose and flooded many low-lying areas. Land masses were separated into islands. Animals, such as the woolly mammoth and reindeer, retreated to the cooler north. The people who lived in Europe had to find new animals to hunt, such as forest deer, ox and pig.

Forest animals did not roam far, so the hunters began to build permanent settlements. One of these was Lepenski Vir on the River Danube, which is one of the earliest settlements in Europe. About 100 people probably lived there, hunting and fishing in the river. There were fifty-nine houses made of wood and stone.

▲ A 'fish god' carved in stone from Lepenski Vir shows the importance of fish in the people's diet. You can see the scales, eyes and mouth of the fish.

▼ The people were buried curled up on their sides, as though asleep.

Near the hearth in most of the houses, the excavators found a strange, round, stone head with thick lips and a down-turned mouth. These may have been images of fish gods which the people worshipped to give thanks for the fish they caught in the river.

Burial Ground at Roonka Flat

Australia, c. 4000–2000 BC

The people who travelled to Australia from Asia about 50,000 years ago developed a lifestyle which remained much the same for thousands of years. The Aboriginals, as they were named by European explorers, found food by hunting and gathering, which allowed them to live successfully in the difficult landscape and climate of Australia.

Early sites like the burial ground at Roonka Flat on the Murray River show how the Aboriginals lived thousands of years ago. There are twelve graves in this earliest example of a burial site in Australia. The bodies were buried upright; each was found with bone or shell jewellery. In later burials, people were buried lying down with offerings such as food and tools.

▲ A pair of skeletons in their burial position. These people might have been roaming Australia while the pyramids were being built in Egypt.

Roonka Flat is named after the roongko grub, which is found in the rotting wood of gum trees. The people who lived there would have found these grubs good to eat.

▼ A close-up of one of the skulls still wearing its shell headdress.

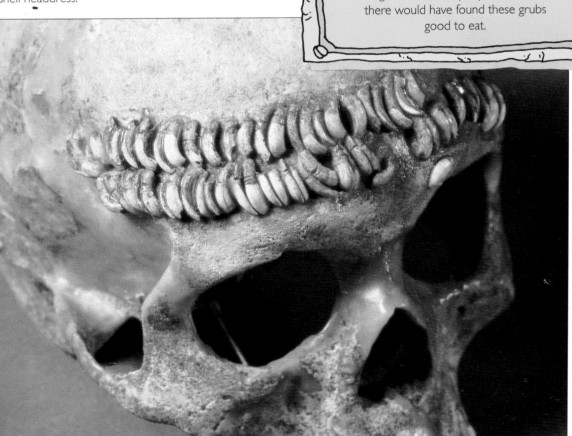

The Na'rmer Palette

Komel-Ahmer, Egypt, 3100 BC

This ancient slate palette was found in the ruins of a temple at Komel-Ahmer in 1898. It is the world's first piece of recorded history and the first example of Egyptian hieroglyphic writing.

   The palette tells of the exploits of Na'rmer, the first pharaoh of Egypt. At this time, Egypt was divided into two parts, Upper and Lower Egypt. Na'rmer, or Menes as he is also known, was the pharaoh of Upper Egypt, but he wanted to conquer Lower Egypt and unite the two halves under his rule.

   The scenes and symbols on the Na'rmer Palette show the pharaoh's struggles in battles with his enemies. On one side, the pharaoh is clubbing an enemy with a stone mace. The pharaoh wears the white crown of Upper Egypt. To the right of the pharaoh is a falcon with text inscribed under it. The text reads 'the god Horus offers the captive delta to the king'. This refers to the delta region of Upper Egypt, which the pharaoh was trying to conquer.

   On the other side of the palette, the victorious pharaoh wears the red crown of Lower Egypt as

▲ The palette is also important because it shows the development of early Egyptian hieroglyphics.

he inspects bodies on a battlefield. At the top is Na'rmer's name in hieroglyphics – a catfish for 'nar' and a chisel for 'mer'. Later pharaohs, such as Rameses II, were keen on advertising their victories with statues and carvings. Perhaps the palette was Na'rmer's way of putting his victories on record.

There may have been kings before the First Dynasty which began with Na'rmer's reign. There is some evidence of a king called Scorpion who may have ruled over Upper Egypt before Na'rmer. But as there is no written evidence, we cannot be sure.

◀ King Menes clubs an enemy in his battle to gain control over the whole of Egypt. The victorious king is said to have founded the first capital of Egypt at Memphis.

The Sumers of Uruk

Iran, c. 3000 BC

The development of the first cities began in Mesopotamia between the rivers Euphrates and Tigris in about 3500 BC. Until then, people had lived in villages, but life was difficult in this region (modern Syria and Iraq) because of the hot climate. Every settlement was near a river, and irrigation schemes were needed to water the fields.

Farming took up a great deal of time, but eventually people began to produce more food than they needed. The surplus food could be traded for such items as tools and pots. Soon the demand for goods increased and foreign trade developed. It then made sense to have centres where people could bring their goods to exchange for others, and from which foreign trade could be controlled.

The city of Uruk in Sumer is one of the

▲ This silver bowl is about 5000 years old, but the figure of the woman looks quite delicate and modern.

▼ The facade of the Temple of Innana at Uruk. The brick statue is the fertility goddess, Ishtar.

The god-king Gilgamesh was the king of Uruk. It was from Uruk that he set out on his legendary journey to learn how to live for ever. This, and other adventures are described in the poem, the *Epic of Gilgamesh*.

earliest cities and many important finds have been made there. By about 3000 BC, it had developed from two settlements and was a large and thriving centre for trade and culture.

The first written tablets were found here and also many fine examples of Sumerian art. The walls of the ceremonial hall were covered with mosaics, and many examples of decorative art were found in the temple complex which dominated the city.

The Village of Skara Brae

Scotland, c. 3000-2500 BC

The Orkney Islands off the north coast of Scotland are cold and windswept. Yet there is evidence that people lived on one of the islands, Orkney Mainland, nearly 5,000 years ago. The settlement, Skara Brae, had been built near the shore, but the people had deserted it thousands of years ago.

It lay hidden under sand dunes until 1850, when a storm blew the sand away and parts of the village could be seen. Archaeologists began to excavate the site, but the main work of uncovering Skara Brae was carried out by Professor Vere Gordon Childe in 1928 and 1929. The village he uncovered had six or seven stone houses. The houses had been solidly built and they even had stone furniture, such as beds and shelf units.

Life was hard for the people of Skara Brae. The weather was so cold that food could not be grown easily. The villagers would have had to spend most of their time looking after their

▲ A necklace made from animal teeth and bone.

animals and searching for food. But work at Skara Brae showed that they also made pots and simple jewellery carved from animal bone. For some reason, the people abandoned Skara Brae in about 2,500 BC. Why they did this remains a mystery that archaeologists cannot solve.

A strange thing is that the abandoned houses at Skara Brae were then filled with rubbish, such as shells and animal bones, which had been arranged in layers. This may have been some sort of religious ritual, but we do not know what it means.

◀ A house at Skara Brae. In the middle of the room is the hearth, surrounded by stones to keep the fire in. The people slept on stone box beds, like the one on the right. Stone slabs round the beds kept out the cold night air. At the back is a storgae unit.

The Boat from the Great Pyramid

Giza, Egypt, c. 2540 BC

The three pyramids at Giza, one of the Seven Wonders of the Ancient World, were built as tombs for three pharaohs: Khufu, Khafre and Menkaure. The Great Pyramid, Khufu's tomb, is the largest of the three.

In the 1950s, a wooden boat was found in a pit near the Great Pyramid. The boat, which had been dismantled before being put into the pit, was made from 1,224 pieces of wood, mainly cedarwood which the Egyptians imported from the Lebanon. When the pieces were put together again, they made a boat 43 m long. So why was a dismantled boat buried near the pharaoh's tomb?

The Egyptians believed in an afterlife which was very similar to life on earth. They thought that they needed all their possessions to use in the afterlife, which is why so many grave goods were put into their tombs. Most tombs contained a model boat for the soul of the dead person to make the journey to the underworld, where the god Osiris ruled. Perhaps Khufu wanted a full-size boat to ensure that he made the journey safely.

▲ King Khufu's boat may have been used during his lifetime for ceremonial journeys during religious festivals.

Khufu reigned for 23 years. It is estimated that during every year of his reign, 100,000 stone blocks were quarried, shaped and taken to the site at Giza to be added to his massive pyramid. No one knows exactly how the blocks were moved into position on the site.

Library of Ebla

Syria, c. 2500 BC

In 1974, archaeologists excavating the ancient city of Ebla found forty-two small clay tablets in a room in the palace. More tablets were discovered in other rooms as the dig continued.

In all, the archaeologists found over 19,000 clay tablets, each covered with cuneiform (wedge-shaped) writing in a language which no one could understand. It was similar to the script used by the Sumerians, which archaeologists could already read, but had many different symbols.

But soon many tablets were found with lists of words in Sumerian and the language of Ebla on them. Once scholars could read them, they found that the tablets formed a library of information about Ebla – the city's history, trade and much more – giving insight into life in Syria 4,500 years ago.

▲ This tablet gives details of taxes to be paid in bread to the governors of the city.

In one room of the palace, archaeologists found a scribe's equipment for writing on the tablets. There were bone stylii for making the symbols, and a stone eraser for removing mistakes.

▼ The library at Ebla, where 19,000 clay tablets were found in the 1970s. The tablets are a record of more than 140 years of the city's history.

Royal Tombs of Ur

Iraq, c. 2500 BC

In the 1920s, the British archaeologist, Sir Leonard Woolley, was excavating the city of Ur when he made a grim discovery. He had found the Royal Cemetery of the ancient kings of Ur, and evidence of a sinister burial practice.

Ur began in about 4500 BC as a small settlement on the banks of the River Euphrates in Mesopotamia. By about 2500 BC, it was a thriving city and the capital of Sumer, southern Mesopotamia.

It was near the ziggurat (pyramid temple) that Woolley found the Royal Cemetery. There were sixteen large tombs, which he called 'death pits' – the graves of the kings and queens of Sumer. However, the royals did not go to their graves alone. They took courtiers and servants with them to the afterlife.

When the king or queen's body had been placed in the burial chamber, a procession of courtiers, servants and musicians went into the death pit. They were dressed in their finest clothes and took gold, jewels and other offerings. Inside the tomb, they drank poison and lay down in orderly rows to die.

▲ This gold and lapis lazuli ram or goat in a bush is the sort of thing the people took into the tombs.

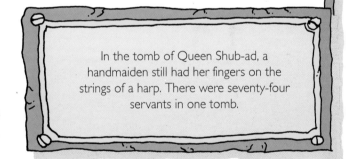

In the tomb of Queen Shub-ad, a handmaiden still had her fingers on the strings of a harp. There were seventy-four servants in one tomb.

▼ The Royal Standard of Ur, found in a royal tomb, is a hollow box. The pictures on the sides illustrating peace and war are made of shell and lapis lazuli.

The Hypogeum

Paola, Malta, c. 2400 BC

In 1902, workmen building a water tank in Paola in Malta made an astonishing discovery. As they cut through the rock, they uncovered a huge underground chamber carved out of the rock.

Archaeologists began to excavate and found a large complex of separate rooms built on three levels. They were excited by the discovery, but also baffled by this Hypogeum (the name comes from a Greek word meaning 'beneath the earth'). The Hypogeum was built in the same style as temples and tombs from the same period on Malta, but it was the only underground structure.

The temples had been built by a Stone Age people who lived on Malta around 2400 BC. Archaeologists found the bones of about 7,000 people, which led them to believe that this was not a temple but a large burial complex.

▼ The temples on Malta are made from large standing stones arranged in circles or ovals. Some of the slabs in the buildings look like altars.

▲ The Sleeping Lady of Hal Saflieni was found in the Hypogeum. She may have been an object of worship.

One room in the Hypogeum is known as the Oracle Chamber. There is a hole in the wall with a space behind. Perhaps people came to consult the oracle and a priest hidden away in this space replied in a voice that echoed eerily round the room.

Mohenjo-Daro

Pakistan, c. 2250 BC

The first civilization in what is now Pakistan developed in the fertile valley of the River Indus. By about 2500 BC, larger cities had appeared. One of these was Mohenjo-Daro, a large city with a population of about 40,000 people.

Mohenjo-Daro was built on a mound with a citadel surrounded by houses. The citadel probably housed religious and official buildings. Many artefacts have been found at the site, including pottery, metalwork and beadwork. Fine seals have also been discovered. These show animals, such as elephants and oxen, and each has an inscription.

The Indus civilization ended in about 2000 BC. At Mohenjo-Daro, this may have happened because the River Indus changed its course, and the fields around the city became too dry for farming.

▲ The buildings and streets of the city were built of baked bricks. The bricks were all the same size, showing they had been made in moulds. Many of the streets had covered drains.

◀ An Indus seal from Mohenjo-Daro, showing a humped bull. Indus seals have been found in Mesopotamia, which suggests that merchants attached them to goods for export. The inscription on each seal may have been the name of the merchant that it belonged to.

The Treasure of Troy

Turkey, c. 2000 BC

In 1870, a German merchant named Hermann Schliemann set out to find the lost city of Troy which the Greek poet Homer had described in the *Odyssey* and the *Iliad*.

Schliemann found the ruins of a fortified citadel which had flourished between 3000 and 1000 BC. One of the legends handed down from the Ancient Greeks was of the amazing hoard of treasure which had belonged to King Priam of Troy. If the city existed, perhaps the treasure did too.

As Schliemann worked on the site, he found that a treasure did exist and had lain there untouched for nearly 3,000 years. He unearthed vast hoards of gold and precious stones. A gold crown was made up of 1,600 separate pieces of gold. There were 9,000 gold rings and buttons and many gold cups and salvers. Schliemann and his wife, Sophie, worked secretly to dig out the treasures and take them back to Europe.

▲ Mrs Schliemann wearing some of the gold jewellery from Troy. It is possible that Schliemann bought it from tomb robbers to beef up his claims about Troy.

After much argument about whether the hoard was really King Priam's lost treasure, it ended up in a museum in Berlin from where it disappeared during the Second World War. In 1995, a museum in Moscow admitted to holding the treasures and promised to put them on display.

▼ A gold vessel from King Priam's treasure which was stolen from a Berlin museum in 1945.

Newgrange Tomb Complex

Ireland, c. 4000 BC

The best evidence of early Irish people comes from the large burial mounds, such as the one at Newgrange, near Drogheda in County Meath.

The mound is surrounded by a circle of stones, some of which are decorated with carvings. A stone passage leads from the entrance of the mound to a network of burial chambers built from large stones.

The chambers are built in a pyramid shape and the sides slope up to a single stone in the roof. Many of the stones in the passage and chambers are also decorated with carvings.

Burial mounds were believed to be entrances to the underworld, and the large ones such as Newgrange were seen as houses of the gods. Ceremonies were probably held there. So the mound was not just a place to bury the dead. It was a focal point of the whole community.

The Newgrange mound is circular, about 90 m in diameter and about 15 m high. They were probably built by the ordinary people at times when there was no farming going on.

▼ The entrance to the tomb at Newgrange. The entrance slab has been carved with a design of spirals and four-sided shapes.

Otzi, the Iceman

Italy, c. 2000 BC

In September 1991, a German couple on holiday in the Italian Alps made an astonishing discovery. They were experienced mountaineers and explored routes which others rarely tackled. While returning to a mountain hut after tackling the summit of Finailspitze mountain, they made their discovery – the top part of a body sticking out of the ice. Little did they know that the body had been there for 4,000 years.

The body, nicknamed Otzi, had been mummified by the ice and was examined by experts. It was dated by objects found with it, such as flint tools and an axe with a metal head. The shape of the axe head was common in the early Bronze Age. The objects and the iceman's clothing, all preserved by the ice, give fascinating information about life in the Bronze Age.

▲ The sight the German couple saw – the man's head and upper body were sticking out of the ice which had preserved it for nearly 4,000 years.

▼ The man was carrying a bow and a quiver containing arrows, and also fire-making equipment.

The iceman had been wounded by an arrow and also had a leg injury. It is possible that he was a criminal fleeing from justice or a fugitive escaping a raid on his village by a neighbouring tribe. Either way, his decision to climb the pass proved fatal.

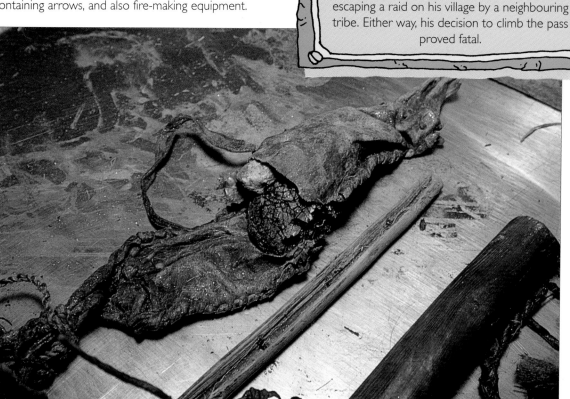

Hammurabi's Law Code

Iraq, c. 1800 BC

Warring city-states were always vying for power in Mesopotamia, and different cities had a period when they were powerful. One of the periods when Babylon dominated the area was the reign of King Hammurabi (1792–50 BC).

Because his subjects had many different ideas and had often been at war with one another, Hammurabi drew up a set of laws for the people to follow. This is one of the earliest written sets of laws to have survived.

There were 282 laws including criminal laws and laws about owning slaves, marriage and divorce, getting into debt and paying wages. Some of the laws sound very sensible: Law 233 says, 'If a builder builds a house ... and does not make his work perfect ... that builder shall put [it] into sound condition at his own cost.'

▲ Hammurabi's Laws were carved on a stele or pillar. At the top is a carving of Hammurabi with Sameth, the Babylonian god of justice.

▼ A carving of Hammurabi. As well as setting out his laws, he established one Babylonian religion instead of the worship of many different gods.

Punishments were harsh. One law states, 'If a man has put out the eye of a free man, they shall put out his eye.' However, putting out the eye of a slave was not so bad – the punishment for that was a fine.

Palace Murals

Mari, Iraq, c. 1750 BC

The palace of Mari was the largest in Mesopotamia in this period. It was built of mud brick and had more than 300 rooms arranged around an inner courtyard. Next to the palace was the temple complex. Much of our evidence about life in Mesopotamia comes from palaces such as the one at Mari.

Mari was a prosperous city from 2500 BC to about 1750 BC, which was a respectable 750 years. The palace dates from the reign of King Zimri-Lim (c. 1775–60 BC). Archaeologists have found murals which decorated the walls of the courtyard and the main rooms.

The murals were painted on plaster. One of them shows a procession of people leading bulls to be sacrificed as part of a religious ritual. There were also

decorations of shell mosaics like the one in the picture below. This style of decoration had been popular during the earlier Sumerian period (see page 29).

About 17,500 clay tablets have also been found. These give details of life in the palace and the city. Mari's wealth seems to have come from collecting tolls from ships on the River Euphrates, and from farming. Water was brought to the fields by canals and there were very extensive irrigation works.

The tablets tell us that royal ladies played an important part in royal life. They held the keys to the storerooms and also controlled many of the palace officials.

▼ A picture of a chariot, from the palace at Mari. The design is inlaid mother of pearl.

The Sun Chariot

Trundholm, Denmark, c. 1650 BC

Most ancient people worshipped a sun god. They realized that the sun was necessary for life and they prayed and made sacrifices to their sun gods to make sure that the sun rose each day.

This Sun Chariot was discovered in a bog at Trundholm in Zealand, Denmark. It dates back to the Bronze Age and shows that the people who were then living in that region almost certainly worshipped a sun god. The model is made of bronze and shows a horse pulling a disc which is gold on one side. The disc probably represents the sun.

Why was it found in a bog? Many bronze items have been found in bogs in Scandinavia, and they were probably put there as religious offerings.

The Bronze Age began in Europe in about 2300 BC. Before this time metalworkers had used copper, silver or gold to make ornaments and other objects. Bronze is a mixture of copper and tin, and neither metal is found in Scandinavia. They had to be imported which made bronze rare and expensive. The Bronze Age lasted until about 1000 BC, when the Iron Age began.

▼ The Sun Chariot was probably an object of worship dedicated to a sun god. Other rituals centred on bogs and lakes were concerned with earth and water gods.

In many mythologies, the sun chariot was supposed to carry the sun across the sky and down into the underworld at the end of the day. However, no one knows what the people of Zealand believed in those days as they had no way of writing down their beliefs.

Oracle Bones

An-yang, China, c. 1500 BC

The origins of Chinese history were shrouded in mystery until the end of the nineteenth century when a Chinese expert in ancient script managed to decipher inscriptions on 'oracle bones'. These were animal bones which had been used by soothsayers more than a thousand years earlier to look into the future. The bones gave us important information about life under the Shang dynasty, who governed the country from about 1500 BC. From the writing on the bones, we now know that the people of the Shang dynasty invented the first form of Chinese writing. The Shang capital of An-yang in northern China was finally excavated between 1927 and 1936.

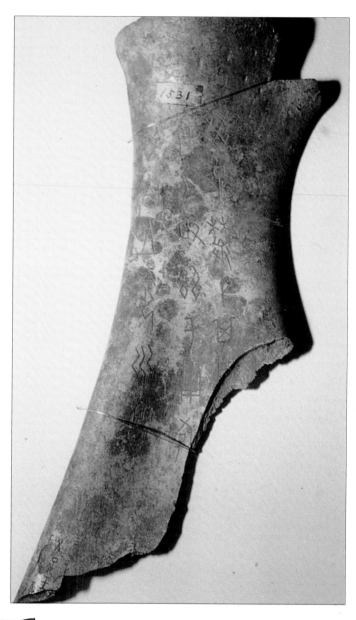

▲ An oracle bone used by a soothsayer in ancient China. Inscriptions on these bones give us some evidence about the Shang dynasty.

Human bones found at the Shang capital at An-yang tell us that people were sacrificed in religious rituals. Archaeologists also found vessels for offering food and wine to the spirits of ancestors, which has always remained the basis of Chinese religion.

Palace of Minos

Knossos, Crete, c. 1500 BC

The island of Crete lies at the southern end of the Aegean Sea. By 2500 BC, it had become the home of the Minoan civilization. The Minoans – named after their legendary king, Minos – were peaceful people who loved art and beauty, and also built up trade links around the Mediterranean.

People knew very little about the Minoans until the English archaeologist, Sir Arthur Evans, uncovered the ruins of a magnificent palace at Knossos in 1900. In the ruins of the palace, Evans found a wealth of artefacts. He found gold jewellery and ornaments and skilfully decorated pottery and statues.

There were also brilliantly coloured wall paintings with magnificent likenesses of birds and animals, many of them sea creatures, which illustrated the Minoans' link with the sea.

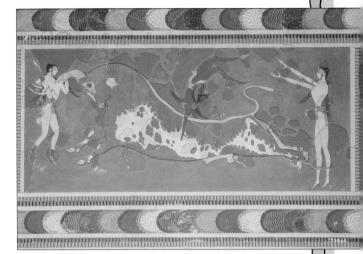

▲ A fresco showing bull-leaping from Knossos. At this religious ritual, young athletes grasped a bull's horns and somersaulted over its back to please the earth-bull god, Poseidon.

Evans also found tablets with writing on them in two styles, Linear A and Linear B. No one could understand the writing until an English schoolboy, Michael Ventris, began to study Linear B. After ten years of study, Ventris managed to decipher the writing.

◀ Storage jars for keeping grain and other foods at the palace.

Fortress of Agamemnon

Mycenae, Greece, c. 1400 BC

In the late nineteenth century, a German archaeologist, Heinrich Schliemann, set out to find the Mycenaean fortress which Homer had talked about in his epic poem, the *Odyssey*. He found the lost town in 1876. So who were the Mycenaeans?

The first Greek-speaking peoples began to invade what is now the Greek mainland in about 2000 BC. These people became known as the Mycenaeans. They built palaces such as the one at Mycenae, and became a fabulously rich and successful civilization.

When Schliemann excavated the royal tombs at Mycenae, he found amazing quantities of gold. There were gold death masks for kings, crowns and jewellery for their queens, and bowls, cups and daggers, all made of gold. And they might never have been found if Homer had not written about these people 500 years after they disappeared, and if Schliemann had not followed up the clues and found the lost fortress of Agamemnon.

▲ A gold death mask, the so-called 'Mask of Agamemnon', found in a shaft grave within the walls of the fortress, suggesting that it was a king's tomb.

The Mycenaeans developed a civilization which lasted for 400 years. In time, the fortress fell into ruin and became buried, and people began to think that the Mycenaeans had only existed in legend.

◄ This picture from a magazine dated 1877 shows a Victorian artist sketching the Lion Gate, the entrance to Mycenae.

The First Alphabet

Ugarit, Syria, c. 1400 BC

Writing was invented to keep records of trading and business accounts. The earliest forms have been found in Syria, Mesopotamia and Persia (now Iran). The writing was done by making marks on wet clay tablets, using a reed which gave wedge-shaped or cuneiform marks. At first, scribes used hundreds of symbols to write. It was hard to write anything with so many symbols and even more difficult to decipher it.

In about 1400 BC, an alphabet using only thirty symbols was devised. Evidence of this alphabet has been found in Ugarit in Syria. As far as we know, this was the first alphabet to be used. Alphabets were later adopted for the writing of Hebrew, Phoenician and Greek. The Roman alphabet we now use developed from these ancient scripts.

▲ The earliest known alphabet is the cuneiform Ugaritic script which dates from about 1400 BC. These tablets give examples of the symbols used. Other alphabets developed from each other.

Chinese writing was developed independently of other scripts. Unlike other writing, the number of symbols used in Chinese has grown over the years. In AD 100, there were about 9,000 symbols. Today there are about 60,000.

▼ The earliest stories, poems and legends that we know were recorded on clay tablets like this one.

The Tomb of Tutankhamun

Valley of the Kings, Egypt, c. 1340 BC

The ancient Egyptians buried some of their greatest kings, or pharaohs, in the Valley of the Kings. By the early twentieth century, archaeologists had uncovered nearly all of these. Most of the finds were disappointing, because grave robbers had taken all the treasure.

However, a British archaeologist, Howard Carter, believed that there was one tomb still to find – that of the boy king, Tutankhamun. And one morning in November 1922, Carter's team uncovered what they were looking for.

When Carter and the man who had financed Carter's work, Lord Carnarvon, entered the tomb, an extraordinary sight met their eyes. The boy king's tomb had been sealed for over 3,000 years, undiscovered by grave robbers. Everything was in place. There was a chamber full of food, furniture and possessions for the afterlife.

The king was in a separate burial chamber. His body had been placed in three gold coffins, one inside the other. Some 140 pieces of jewellery were placed on his death mask.

▲ Tutankhamun's death mask has a vulture and a cobra on the forehead. These symbols show that he was king of Upper and Lower Egypt.

Tutankhamun's predecessor and father-in-law, Akhenaton, changed the practice of worshipping different gods and introduced a single deity, Aton, the Sun God.
Tutankhamun, who as a young boy appears to have been a puppet in the hands of the priests, returned to the traditional way of worshipping many gods.

◀ A carving on the back of the throne found in Tutankhamun's tombs. It shows the boy king and his wife, Ankhesenpaaten.

Giants' Heads

San Lorenzo, Mexico, 1200–900 BC

The Olmecs, who lived near the east coast of Mexico from about 1300 BC, were the first civilization of Central America. They were skilled artists and sculptors who worked in materials such as jade and basalt, which had to be brought long distances from other parts of Mexico.

The Olmec ceremonial centre at San Lorenzo contains much evidence of their artistry. The centre was built on a natural plateau which is about 50 m high. On the top of the plateau there were several earth platforms around a courtyard. There was a court for a sacred ball game played by many of the peoples of Mexico, and pools for ritual bathing.

The ceremonial centre was decorated with sculptures and carved reliefs, many of which were massive. There were huge carved blocks of basalt which may have been used as thrones, and colossal heads of Olmec rulers. The larger pieces of sculpture had been deliberately damaged in about 900 BC and then buried along the top of the plateau. No one knows why this happened.

There were about 200 house mounds in San Lorenzo, and evidence that the Olmecs were a farming community, growing maize and other crops in the nearby fields.

Many Olmec carvings are in the shape of baby-faced people with snarling, down-turned mouths. These strange creatures may have been rain gods.

◀ These massive heads depicting Olmec rulers are one of the most distinctive forms of Olmec art. The ruler wears a helmet with side straps and a glyph (picture symbol) on the front. The head is made of basalt and is nearly 3 metres high.

Assurbanipal's Library

Nineveh, Iraq, 860 BC

The Assyrians were ruthless invaders who built up a great empire by bloody warfare. When they conquered a new land, they were exceedingly cruel to their new subjects. They put up pillars in the captured states, showing carvings of their bloodthirsty victories to remind people what would happen if the Assyrians were crossed.

But the Assyrians were not just barbaric killers. They built beautiful cities, such as Nineveh, Kalah (modern Nimrud) and Khorsabad. City life was well organized by officials who saw that law and order was maintained.

Assyrian artists made fine carvings and reliefs showing scenes of everyday life, such as the royal lion hunt, when the king and his hunting party would go out to destroy mountain lions which preyed on people and farm animals.

The palace at Nineveh housed the library of King Assurbanipal, the last great Assyrian king. The library consisted of 20,000 clay tablets in cuneiform (see pages 32 and 56), giving records of laws and history.

The *Epic of Gilgamesh*, the poem about the heroic deeds of the god-king, was found on twelve tablets in this library when archaeologists excavated the site in the nineteenth century.

By the end of the seventh century BC, the Assyrians had so many enemies that they could be overthrown by a large-scale invasion. Nineveh was conquered and destroyed in 612 BC. The ancient library of Assurbanipal was buried for centuries amid the ruins of the palace.

▼ This relief from Assurbanipal's library shows the king and queen relaxing as servants fan them. The tablets give us evidence about clothes, furniture and other everyday things, as well as historical facts.

The *Epic of Gilgamesh* tells of the legendary king of Uruk, Gilgamesh, who set out to find the secret of eternal life. Though he was thought to be a god-king, Gilgamesh really did exist. There are records about wars between him and a king of Kish.

Hoards of the Medes

Ziweyeh and Nush-i Jan, Iran, c. 860 BC

The Medes were a group of people who had settled in what is now western Iran in the mid ninth century BC. They probably came from various different tribes who joined together for greater strength against the Assyrians, who were raiding Persia, now Iran. By the seventh century BC, the Medes had managed to gain control over a wide area, which they ruled from their capital, Ecbatana (modern-day Hamadan).

There is not much evidence about the Medes, and most of the finds are in pottery. A hoard of gold is claimed to be Median – it is said to have been found at Ziweyeh in north-western Iran – but archaeologists are not sure whether the objects had originally been discovered there or somewhere else.

We know that the art of the people who lived at Ziweyeh was influenced by their neighbours, the Scythians, and the design of the gold objects do show this influence.

▲ This gold head was probably a votive object or symbol of worship from a temple.

Though little is known about the culture of the Medes, we do know that they became powerful and gained control over the lands of the Persians and, later, the Assyrian Empire in Mesopotamia and the Near East.

A silver hoard found at Nush-i Jan provides more definite evidence about the Medes. The silver was probably hidden there in the sixth century BC, though some of the pieces are older than that. The hoard includes several pieces of jewellery, which were probably used for trading in the days before coins were invented.

◄ A gold plaque showing a Scythian warrior in the Persian army. He wears ribbed leather armour and wields a battle-axe.

Temple Complex

Chavin de Huantar, Peru, c. 800–200 BC

The earliest civilization in the Andes Mountains region of Peru was the Chavin, who dominated the area between 1200 and 200 BC. These people were named after their main settlement at Chavin de Huantar, where an impressive temple complex has been found. Chavin de Huantar and its temple complex was well established by 800 BC. The Chavin worshipped animal gods, such as the jaguar, the eagle and the snake, and the temple is honeycombed with rooms where objects of worship were hidden.

One of the objects was the Great Image, a stone carving of a god with a snarling mouth and fearsome fangs. This 4.5-m carving can still be seen in the temple today. Another item, the Staff

God, was a catlike creature with long fangs. Examples of the Chavin's craftsmanship have been found all over their domain. The artefacts are made from pottery, wood, stone, shell, silver or gold, and all are decorated with images of Chavin gods.

By about 200 BC, other peoples living in the Andes Mountains had developed their own cultures. They lived different lives from one another and no longer looked to the Chavin for leadership. The Chavin's domination had ended, but their influence paved the way for future civilizations to take control over this part of South America.

▼ The ceremonial entrance to the temple complex at Chavin de Huantar, where the Chavin would have worshipped their animal gods.

The gods worshipped by the Chavin were adopted by later civilizations. These gods were worshipped, most recently by the Inca peoples, until the arrival of the European invaders in the sixteenth century.

The Celtic Cemetery

Hallstatt, Austria, c. 700–550 BC

About 3,000 years ago, Europe was occupied by Celtic peoples who had developed their own distinctive way of life, or culture. One of the most important finds from this period was the Celtic cemetery at Hallstatt in Austria.

By the sixth century BC, the Celts had established strong trading links with Greek cities around the Mediterranean Sea. Trade made the nobles rich. They became princely in their importance and built hilltop fortresses, which they filled with many fine possessions. Their possessions were later buried with them.

Finds from Hallstatt contained Greek pottery and bronze wine vessels, among many other treasures. These show that the Celtic nobles adopted ideas, such as the habit of drinking wine, from the Greeks.

Graves from the fifth century BC held weapons and chariots and fewer riches. Fighting for land had clearly become more important than trading.

▲ Johann Georg Ramsauer found these treasures in the cemetery at Hallstatt during excavations in the mid-nineteenth century.

Grab 116, Körpergrab

By the third century BC, the Celts had adopted another Greek idea, using coins for trading. The earliest Celtic coins were clearly based on Greek designs, although the copies were not very good.

◀ A Celtic dagger from the cemetery at Hallstatt. People were buried with weapons which were the most important possessions for warriors who were bent on conquest.

Lost Village in the Lake

Biskupin, Poland, c. 600 BC

About 720 BC, a group of people, probably Slavs, arrived on the shores of Lake Biskupin, about 225 kilometres west of present-day Warsaw. They decided to settle and build a village, picking a marshy promontory of about two hectares jutting out into the lake.

About a hundred houses were crammed inside a strong wall with only one gate. The wall was six metres high and three metres thick. The houses were anchored on piles to prevent them from sinking into the swampy ground. The ground between the houses was paved with logs to make it easier to move about.

By about 520 BC, the water level started to rise, the shoreline changed – and eventually the village found itself on the bottom of the lake. But why build a village on such marshy land? Probably because there was not much clear land to build on. The surrounding valleys were covered with dense forests and the villagers needed a supply of fresh water. They could also catch fish from the lake. So, although there must have been difficulties, their choice made sense.

▼ Neat rows of wooden houses at Biskupin were surrounded by a strong wooden defensive wall.

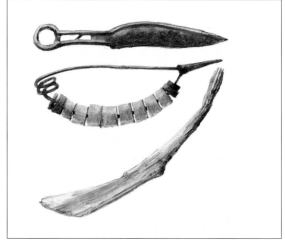

▲ Archaeologists at Biskupin unearthed bronze items such as knives and pins. Some wooden objects, such as a plough, were preserved in the water.

The drowned Neolithic village in Lake Zürich was unknown until the winter of 1853–4, when the level of the lake fell and some wooden poles were seen sticking out of the water. A similar underwater village was discovered in Lake Paladru in France. The people had used flint axes to chop down trees to build their houses.

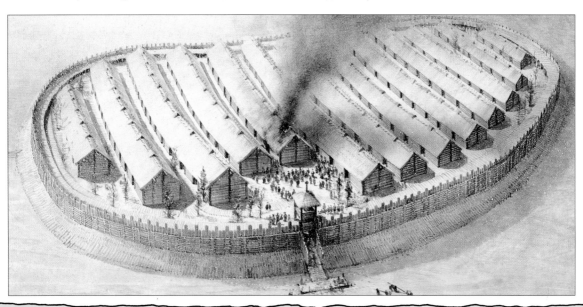

The Explorers of the Pacific

Fiji and Tonga, c. 600 BC

In about 1500 BC, the Lapita people could be found over a wide range of Pacific islands, from the Admiralty Islands in the west to Tonga in the east. The Lapita were skilled navigators, taking their canoes all over the Pacific. Archaeologists have found many items which tell us about their culture.

The Lapita made tools from a hard, volcanic stone called obsidian. They also made intricately designed pottery and ornaments from shells. One of their most interesting achievements was a navigation chart which they made from sea shells attached to a framework of sticks. The shells represented the position of the islands and the chart also showed currents and swells.

▲ Charts made of shells and sticks were used to train Lapita sailors to navigate to islands in the Pacific.

▼ The areas now known as Melanesia and western Polynesia were settled by the Lapita people some 3,500 years ago.

No one knows exactly where the Polynesian people came from originally, but their astonishing ocean voyages have allowed them to spread right across the Pacific. They colonized from the Caroline Islands in the west to Easter Island in the east and from Hawaii to New Zealand.

PHILIPPINES

MICRONESIA

MELANESIA

NEW GUINEA

Hawaiian Islands

Samoa

Fiji

New Caledonia

Tonga

Tahiti

AUSTRALIA

NEW ZEALAND

c 1500 BC
1000 BC – AD 1
Exploration zones
Lapita settlement •

Kostomskaya Barrow

Steppes Nomads, Kuban region, c. 550 BC

The people who lived on the Russian steppes until quite recently were nomads, who moved from place to place to find pasture for their animals. But they were well-organized and some were very wealthy. Most of what we know about the Steppes nomads comes from excavations of burial sites, such as the Kostomskaya Barrow in the Kuban region just to the north-east of the Black Sea.

This was probably the tomb of a chief. He had been buried in a wooden chamber with a high roof over which earth had been piled to form the barrow. Thirteen people, probably his servants, had been buried with the man.

Twenty-two horses had also been put into the grave, showing that the man was rich and important. His grave goods included an iron shield, spearheads and arrowheads. He was probably the leader of a group of powerful warriors who fought on horseback.

▲ Two Scythians (see opposite) drink from a horn. This may be part of a ceremony that makes the two men blood brothers.

▼ This Scythian saddle cover is richly decorated in felt of different colours. It came from a burial mound.

The Steppe nomads were fierce warriors who made invasions into China, India and Europe. If their leader was strong, the Steppe warriors were unbeatable. The man in the Kostomskaya Barrow may have been one of these invincible leaders.

Tattooed Chieftain

Pazyryk, Siberia, c. 500 BC

Archaeologists have uncovered tools, weapons and other possessions which give us an idea of the culture of the Iron Age peoples (started c. 1100 BC). Sites have been found which give clues about Iron Age forts and dwellings. But these discoveries do not tell us much about personal decoration and clothing.

Then, in 1948 a Russian archaeologist opened a burial chamber dating back to about 500 BC and found the bodies of a man and his wife, who were members of a Steppe Nomad people called the Scyths. The tomb was in the steppes of Siberia where the weather is icy cold, and the couple had been frozen for 2,500 years. As a result, their bodies had not broken down, nor decomposed, and their clothes had not rotted away. The man's body was covered with tattoos showing mythical monsters.

▲ This wall hanging shows a Scythian horseman. The Scyths used horses for transport and in warfare in the Steppes of Siberia.

▼ A tattoo from the skin of a Scythian chieftain. The Scyths apparently thought that such tattoos gave them strength in battle.

In the tomb were the bodies of several horses, a sign that the man had been the leader of a nomadic people and used to riding into battle.

Behistun Rock

Iran, c. 490 BC

Cuneiform, named after the Latin word for 'wedge', is one of the earliest forms of writing. The characters were made by pressing a wedge-shaped stick into soft clay in a variety of patterns to form symbols. Cuneiform was developed by ancient civilizations in Mesopotamia (now Iraq) and Persia (now Iran).

However, for hundreds of years after these civilizations had died out, people did not realize that cuneiform was a style of writing and, even if they had realized it, they certainly could not have worked out what it meant.

No one could translate cuneiform until, in the 1830s, an English army officer, Henry Rawlinson, found a wall of carvings at Behistun Rock in western Iran. He climbed the cliff and copied the inscriptions. It took him several years before he managed to decipher them.

▲ Rawlinson's studies helped scholars to decipher the many clay tablets and inscriptions found in Iran and Iraq.

The rock contained inscriptions in three ancient languages – Old Persian, Elamite and Old Babylonian. All were written in cuneiform script. The earliest carvings were made for kings of the Achaemenid dynasty (c. 550–330 BC), but Parthian kings (c. 240 BC–AD 226) also used the site.

▼ The god, Ahura-Mazda, floats in his chariot above the king who is reviewing prisoners taken in battle from various different tribal groups.

Statue of Zeus

Cape Artemesion, Greece, c. 460 BC

In about 900 BC, the Greeks began to build up trade links around the Mediterranean. People had more money and some villages grew into towns and then into city-states. The way was set for the Classical period in Greek history, which was one of the greatest periods in early western civilization. The arts flourished, and the Greeks filled their temples with beautiful statues.

When the Romans conquered the Greeks, they took many Greek works of art back to Rome. One of these was a bronze statue of the king of the gods, Zeus, although some people think it shows Poseidon, the god of the sea. But the statue was lost in a shipwreck off Cape Artemesion, a promontory on the Greek mainland, where it was found hundreds of years later.

▼ Along with many other works of art, the Romans took this fine bronze statue from a Greek temple during the second century BC.

In the cities of ancient Greece, especially Athens, learning also developed during this period. Philosophers, such as Socrates, Plato and Aristotle, discussed ideas, and wrote many books which are still studied to this day.

Zhou Tomb Treasures

Yangzi Valley, China, c. 450 BC

The Shang dynasty, the earliest ruling power in China, was conquered by another strong family, the Zhou, in about 1122 BC. The Zhou came from the valley of the Wei, a river that ran into the Yellow River. They founded a dynasty which lasted for 800 years.

During their dynasty, the Zhou were often challenged – rival states were constantly fighting each other to gain power. This rivalry ended in the Warring States period which lasted from 403 to 226 BC, and ended when the Qin dynasty replaced the Zhou.

Despite the unrest during the second half of their dynasty, the Zhou continued to make an important contribution to Chinese civilization, particularly in the fields of art and philosophy.

Most of what we know about life in China during this period comes from the tombs of Zhou kings and wealthy nobles, particularly those from the Yangzi Valley. The tombs contained many possessions which show the skill of craftworkers at the time, including sculptures in bronze and silver, painted wooden figures, musical instruments, lacquerwork and delicate paintings on silk. These items give a vivid picture of the rich lifestyle enjoyed by wealthy people at this time.

▲ This Zhou carving of a deer is made of wood. The craftsman decorated it with rich lacquers in black and gold.

The power of the Zhou finally ended when the Qin dynasty took over in 226 BC. Their first ruler, Qin Shi Huangdi, chose a name meaning 'first emperor' because he was the first person to bring all the Chinese states under a single leader.

Nok Settlements

Nigeria, c. 450 BC

The Nok people lived in northern Nigeria, near the Niger and Benue rivers, from about 500 BC to the early centuries of this era. It is from this group of people that we get the first evidence of ironworking in Africa.

In most parts of the world, metal working began with copper, because it is softer and easier to melt and mould than iron. So the Copper and Bronze Ages came after the Stone Age, with the Iron Age following on later.

In many parts of Africa, however, the Iron Age followed straight on from the Stone Age – the people had discovered how to make a furnace that was hot enough to melt the iron ore. From the iron they made strong and efficient tools and weapons. Iron-smelting furnaces dating back to about 450 BC have been found at Taruga, a Nok settlement.

Also found at Nok settlements are terracotta heads, some of which are life size. The heads have been modelled in great detail, showing even the people's skin blemishes. We do not know what the purpose of these heads was, but they may have been used for religious rituals.

Early African furnaces could reach 1100°C, the temperature needed to smelt iron. To do this they had to burn massive amounts of charcoal in funnel or dome-shaped structures.

◀ This fine terracotta head, some 36 cm high, is a typical example of the art of the Nok people.

Gold of Persepolis

Iran, c. 400 BC

The Persian empire reached its peak under Darius I, who built the palace at Persepolis starting in 515 BC. He chose a lonely place miles from anywhere – his capital at Susa was a noisy, bustling city; Darius could escape to Persepolis to relax. Every year, officials came from every corner of the empire to celebrate new year at Persepolis. They brought the emperor gifts of precious metals, jewels, weapons and carpets.

Persepolis remained the Persian emperors' country palace until Alexander the Great conquered Persia for Greece in 330 BC. He had the palace burned to the ground and the ruins were buried under sand until archaeologists began to excavate the site in the 1920s. They found the foundations of the palace, together with many sculptures and gold treasures.

▲ A finely decorated gold drinking cup was one of the many treasures found at Persepolis. A gift for the emperor, it was stored in the royal treasury.

Persepolis was a long way from all the other towns and cities of the Persian empire, so the emperor had a network of roads built so that people could travel there. This was a great achievement at a time when there were few roads and most people travelled very little.

▼ The stairs at Persepolis were decorated with carved reliefs showing the tribute processions arriving at the palace to celebrate New Year.

The Enigmatic Etruscans

Pyrgi, Italy c. 350 BC

The Etruscans came from Etruria in the northern and western parts of Italy, and their civilization influenced the Romans who conquered them in 200 BC. They were superb craftsmen and their burial grounds contain many valuable treasures.

The Etruscans were a rich nation who traded around the Mediterranean. They were brave warriors and their cities were modelled on the Greek city-states. But we know very little else about them because no one has managed to translate the Etruscan inscriptions that have been found. The longest of these are on three gold tablets, discovered in 1964 at Pyrgi, near Rome.

Scholars have managed to work out some of the words. But they have not found anything which allows them to compare the Etruscan language with another language which they can understand like Behistun or the Rosetta Stone. Maybe one day someone will find the key to unravel the mysteries surrounding these people.

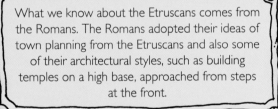

What we know about the Etruscans comes from the Romans. The Romans adopted their ideas of town planning from the Etruscans and also some of their architectural styles, such as building temples on a high base, approached from steps at the front.

▲ The alphabet used on the tablets is similar to Greek, but the language is quite different.

▼ The Etruscans are famous for their bronze sculptures. These examples show a horse race in which the riders dismount and run for part of it.

Tomb of Philip II

Verginia, Macedonia, 336 BC

Philip II, the father of Alexander the Great, came to the throne of Macedon, a wild mountainous area in northern Greece, in 359 BC. He wanted to conquer new lands from Persia and Alexander shared his ambition, but Philip was killed before he could fulfil his aim. Alexander went on to conquer an empire for Greece.

In 1977, a Greek archaeologist, Professor Manolis Andronikos, unearthed a tomb. Inside were many objects scattered around on the floor, including a royal headband, a sword and a solid gold box with a 'sunburst' design on its lid. Professor Andronikos knew that the sunburst was the sign of Macedonia, so the tomb must belong to one of its kings. But which one?

Among the many treasures was a simple pair of bronze leg guards. One leg guard was shorter than the other and it was recorded that Philip had been lamed in battle. Professor Andronikos knew whose tomb he had found.

▲ The stone chest, or sarcophagus, for the body was at one end of the tomb. Grave goods lay around.

▼ The entrance to the tomb.

Alexander the Great conquered an enormous empire. It reached as far east as the River Indus in what is now Pakistan. But the great empire was difficult to hold together, and fell apart after Alexander's death in 323 BC as his warring generals claimed their share.

Topeths of Baal Hammon

Carthage, Tunisia, c. 310 BC

The ancient city of Carthage in North Africa was founded by merchants from the Phoenician city of Tyre. The Carthaginians were the dominant power in the Mediterranean until their defeat by the Romans (see page 65).

Two centuries before this happened, Agathocles, the tyrant ruler of the Sicilian city-state of Syracuse, came to Carthage. He was eyewitness to a horrific event which was later retold by the Greek historian, Diodorus Siculus.

Agathocles reported seeing the ritual burning of 500 children as an offering to the god Baal Hammon. A fire was built in a pit in front of a massive statue of the god and the children were put into the flames.

The children had to be sons and daughters of the nobility. At one time, the nobles had tried to save their children by using the children of slaves, but defeat in battle had followed and they believed this was because Baal Hammon was angry.

There is evidence that this ghastly ritual killing of children was carried out regularly. Archaeologists have discovered the sites of temples and topeths (large furnaces with altars), and in both they found large quantities of bones.

As the war with the Romans became more desperate, the Carthaginians must have tried to appease Baal Hammon with many sacrifices. But in 146 BC, the Romans burned Carthage to the ground and took her lands and people into their expanding empire.

▼ A large number of children's bones were found in this temple, which was probably the scene of several sacrificial ceremonies.

We do not know a great deal about the Carthaginians' religion, but they did worship an Earth Mother called Tanit, to whom they probably sacrificed small animals. There were several gods called Baal; one is named in the Old Testament as a rival to Jehovah.

Oxyrhyncus Papyri

Alexandria, Egypt, c. 305 BC–c. AD 200

Egypt came under Persian rule in 525 BC. In 332 BC, Persia surrendered to Alexander the Great and Egypt became part of the Greek empire. Alexander began work on the city that was named after him, but he died in 323 BC, before he could take over the administration of the country. One of his generals, Ptolemy, declared himself the pharaoh in 305 BC, and started a long line of Ptolemies which ended with Cleopatra, who died in 30 BC. Egypt then became part of the Roman Empire.

Much evidence about Egypt under Greek and Roman rule was found when two British scholars, Bernard Grenfell and Arthur Hunt, excavated the ancient site of Oxyrhynchus. They began work in 1895 and spent ten years on the project, during which they found many ancient papyri (documents written on papyrus).

The papyri included legal documents, letters, petitions and receipts, which all gave important information about the Greek and Roman way of life. There were also copies of lost works by classical authors and scholars, such as Plato, Sophocles and Aristotle. All in all, the papers provided a unique insight into this period in Egyptian history.

▲ A mummy cover from a burial of the Roman period in ancient Egypt.

▼ A performance of the play, *Oedipus Rex*, by Sophocles in an original Greek theatre. Several of Sophocles' works were found among the papyri at Oxyrhynchus.

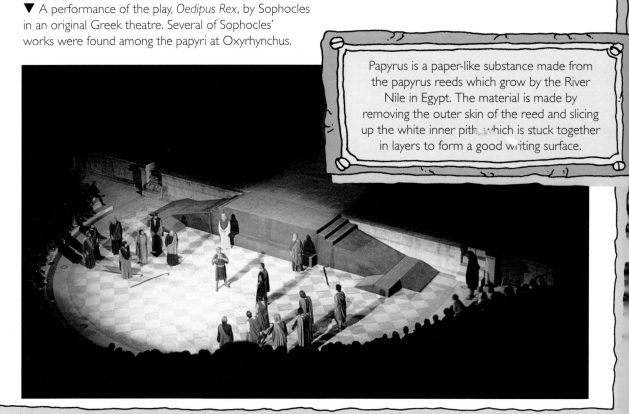

Papyrus is a paper-like substance made from the papyrus reeds which grow by the River Nile in Egypt. The material is made by removing the outer skin of the reed and slicing up the white inner pith, which is stuck together in layers to form a good writing surface.

The Lady of Elche

Spain, c. 300 BC

During the seventh century BC, Rome began to develop from a small settlement to a large city. At this time, the Etruscans were the dominant power in Italy, but as their influence began to decline, the Romans took over. By 250 BC, the Romans controlled the whole of Italy, and were turning their attention to building an empire.

At this time, Carthage in North Africa had established strong trading links all around the Mediterranean Sea. By the fourth century BC, it was the wealthiest city in the area and had expanded enormously. The Carthaginians were looking for more power and so were the Romans. There were bound to be clashes.

The struggle between the two powers as each tried to establish dominance in the Mediterranean led to the Punic Wars, so called because Punicus was the Roman name for the Carthaginians. These wars lasted for over a hundred years, but the Romans gradually took over power from the Carthaginians and they finally conquered Carthage itself in 146 BC.

Spain had been a Carthaginian colony and the Lady of Elche, a painted limestone bust found at La Alcudia de Elche in Spain, is an example of their influence. The Lady wears rich, ornate jewellery in Carthaginian style. But the influence was to change now as Spain became part of the Roman Empire.

The Carthaginian general, Hannibal, made a famous march through Spain and across the Alps into Italy with 60,000 men and thirty-seven elephants to attack the Romans by surprise. He defeated them twice, but, refused support by politicians at home, failed to complete the conquest. Recalled to Africa, his defeat at Zama in 202 BC left Carthage at Rome's mercy.

▶ The limestone bust of the Lady of Elche, found at La Alcudia de Elche in Spain.

The 'Janus' Head

Roquepertuse, France, c. 300 BC

Greek writers mention the Celts of Europe as being tall, fair people who enjoyed drinking wine and fighting. By about 500 BC, the Celtic tribes were ruled by nobles who were always at war with one another. Much of their art went into making and decorating bronze weapons, shields and helmets for war.

However, religion was also an important part of Celtic life and art. The Celts are known to have worshipped many gods and goddesses. They placed their images in shrines like the one at Roquepertuse in southern France. Like much of their culture, Celtic religion was a mixture of bloodthirstiness and art, but not a lot is known about the details of the ceremonies.

▲ Celtic artists also carved beautiful reliefs, like this sculpture of horses' heads, also found at Roquepertuse in southern France.

The Celts sacrificed cattle and human beings to their gods, as well as putting valuable offerings into lakes and bogs. Religious rituals were conducted by powerful priests, such as the Druids who carried out the human sacrifices. It was said the Druids could look into the future.

▼ Carvings like this are called 'Janus' heads after the Roman god, but they are not portraits of him. Janus was often shown with two or three heads – he was the god of the changing year, hence January.

Pataliputra

India, c. 250 BC

By about 600 BC, towns and cities had been built on the plains of the Ganges river. Northern India was divided into sixteen small states which eventually became one large state called Magadha. The Mauryan empire was built up first by Chandragupta Maurya, who came to the throne in 321 BC. His grandson, Asoka, finally ruled over the whole of India.

The Mauryan capital was Pataliputra, a large city on the Ganges. Asoka became a Buddhist and formed strong ideas about how people should behave and lead their lives. His beliefs and laws were carved on rocks and pillars throughout India. From these we can see how wide an area Asoka ruled over at the height of Mauryan power.

▶ This statue of a goddess comes from the period of the Mauryan empire.

▼ Asoka set up pillars all over India, on which the emperor's laws, and details of his Buddhist beliefs were written.

The civilization of India dates back to the great cities of Harappa and Mohenjo-daro, which were established in the Indus Valley by about 2500 BC. But the two cities were abandoned in about 1750 BC, and the centre of Indian civilization took a different turn.

The Terracotta Army

Mount Li, China, 210 BC

▲ This soldier wears scale armour, which is made up of small squares of bronze held together by rivets.

Shi Huangdi was a member of the powerful Qin dynasty from western China. A ruthless man, he conquered all the Chinese states in 210 BC and became the first emperor of China. But though the separate states became united under his leadership, barbarian invaders from the north threatened the empire. So Shi Huangdi built the Great Wall of China.

But, for all his might, the emperor had one great fear – death. Not long after becoming emperor, he began to plan his tomb and 700,000 workers started work on it. He insisted that his tomb should be in a huge pit guarded by about 600,000 life-size pottery soldiers. The army lay forgotten for centuries until, about twenty years ago, a party of Chinese labourers discovered a few statues while digging a well near Mount Li in northern China.

Archaeologists began to excavate the area and, in 1974, they uncovered the secret army of Shi Huangdi. Part of the site remains to be excavated, so more may be found.

▼ Each soldier in the terracotta army has a different face. They must have been portraits of the men in the emperor's real army.

When Shi Huangdi built the Great Wall of China to keep out his enemies, many workers died in the harsh conditions of mountainous northern China. But they succeeded in building the longest structure on earth – and in keeping out the barbarians.

The Gundestrup Cauldron

Denmark, c. 200 BC

There have been many spectacular bog finds – the Celtic peoples of northern Europe used bogs as a place to make offerings to the gods – of which one of the most incredible is the enormous silver cauldron found in a bog in Gundestrup, northern Denmark in 1891.

The cauldron measures 97 cm in diameter and is an excellent example of Celtic workmanship. It is thought that at least three artists worked on it. The inside is decorated with scenes from Celtic mythology and the outside shows various Celtic gods. For example, the horned god, Cerunnos, is shown with stag's antlers and is surrounded by animals, including a stag. He grasps a serpent in his left hand. The Gundestrup Cauldron is one of the most prized pieces of Celtic art ever discovered.

▲ The figures on the Gundestrup cauldron include several of the Celtic gods. The vessel was probably used in religious ceremonies before being buried as an offering to the gods.

The Celts believed that their gods and goddesses could take the form of any animal. This is why creatures of many kinds appear on the cauldron and on other examples of Celtic art that have been found.

▼ The horses on the cauldron wear typical Celtic harness, adorned with rich ornaments.

The Rosetta Stone

Rashid, Egypt, 196 BC

About 5,000 years ago, the ancient Egyptians invented a form of picture writing called hieroglyphs. This method of writing was slow to produce and difficult to understand, and so, about 3,400 years ago, the Egyptians developed a style which was quicker and easier to use.

In time the Egyptians forgot how to read the hieroglyphs. It may well have proved impossible for archaeologists to decipher the writing had it not been for a discovery by French scholars accompanying Napoleon's army, which had invaded Egypt.

In 1799, they uncovered a slab of black rock with writing on it. The text was written in three types of script: Greek, Egyptian hieroglyphs and the later form of Egyptian writing. A French scholar of ancient languages, Jean Paul Champollion, studied the writing, and managed to translate the hieroglyphs.

▲ The Rosetta Stone proved to be the key to translating the hieroglyphs because it contains the same text in three scripts.

Champollion translated the hieroglyphs by comparing the words on the stone and managed to pick out the hieroglyphs for Ptolemy, the last family of pharaohs. He then managed to decipher the meaning of other hieroglyphs. Champollion went on to publish his findings in 1822.

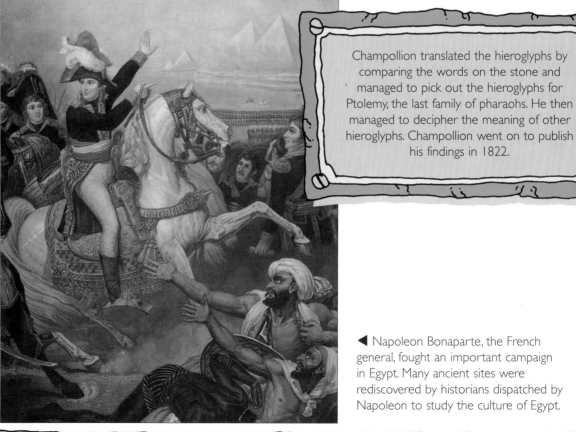

◄ Napoleon Bonaparte, the French general, fought an important campaign in Egypt. Many ancient sites were rediscovered by historians dispatched by Napoleon to study the culture of Egypt.

Tomb of the Marchioness of Dai

Mawangdui, China, c. 150 BC

The Han ruled from 206 BC to AD 220. The tombs of rulers and nobles give us a picture of how the well-off lived – they believed that they had to take their possessions to the afterlife, so they were buried with everything they might need.

One of the most spectacular finds was the tomb of the wife of the Marquis of Dai, who was buried at Mawangdui in the kingdom of Changsha. The Marquis of Dai was the prime minister and his importance is reflected in his wife's tomb. She lay at the centre of a large wooden chamber covered by a 16-m mound of earth.

She had been dressed in twenty layers of clothing and buried in four coffins, each one smaller than the last. She was surrounded by hundreds of possessions, to ensure a happy life in the next world.

▼ Massive stone animals guarded the tombs of the Han dynasty rulers in Shansi, China.

▲ Wall paintings in the tombs of the Han dynasty show a variety of animals and scenes from the everyday life of the time.

Though the Marchioness had been dead for over 2,000 years, her body was well preserved because her tomb was sealed with white clay, keeping out pollution and the weather – as well as robbers.

Antikythera Mechanism

Cape Artemesion, Greece, c. 80 BC

In 1900 a group of sponge divers discovered the wreck of a ship not far from the island of Crete. The ship, which had been carrying a cargo of magnificent statues, including the Zeus, had been lying on the sea-bed since about 80 BC. The ship was recovered and its treasures were sent to the National Archaeological Museum in Athens.

A museum archaeologist was looking through a collection of bronze and marble pieces when he came across a strange object. It was a clock-like mechanism, later called the Antikythera mechanism. Further study showed that it had been made in the first century BC. But what was it? People argued for years about what it was for, and whether the Greeks could have invented it.

Then, in 1975, a professor from Yale University in the USA came up with the answer. The mechanism was made in 87 BC and used to measure the movement of the sun, moon and planets. This was remarkable, for the ancient Greeks did not know about the solar system – they believed that the earth was a circular disc with a dome-shaped sky above it.

> What made the mechanism even more astonishing was that the ancient Greeks were not thought to have the knowledge to make a mechanism of this kind. The Yale professor described discovering the Antikythera mechanism in the ancient shipwreck as like 'finding a jet plane in King Tutankhamun's tomb'!

▼ This complex system of gears and gauges enabled Greek sailors to navigate by plotting the movements of the Sun, Moon and stars.

Trepanned Skull

Peru, c. 50 BC

Could prehistoric people carry out brain surgery? It sounds a ridiculous idea, but a discovery made in the 1860s suggests that they could.

The skull of a Stone Age man was found in Peru. A neat piece had been removed from the skull by cutting two thin parallel grooves and then crossing these with two more grooves. The piece must have been removed to show the brain. This system of bone cutting later came to be known as trepanning.

But what were these early surgeons trying to do? There were to be no pain-killing drugs for thousands of years, so the patient would have been in a lot of pain during the operation.

We can get an idea about Stone Age surgery from trepanning carried out by modern-day tribes. When someone has a head wound, they cut away the bone to tidy it up and remove any loose pieces of bone. As Stone Age peoples had no sharp knives, they probably scraped away at the wound with stone blades.

Horrific though this sounds, many people seemed to have survived the ordeal. A skull found at Cuzco in Peru had seven trepanning holes in it, showing that the person involved had been unlucky with his head wounds, but had been treated successfully each time.

◄ This man's skull has three trepanning holes. The hole at the front has healed so the man survived the first operation. But the other two holes have not healed and he died soon after the third operation.

Archaeologists believe Stone Age people also carried out trepanning to free evil spirits from the heads of people who were feeling depressed or had a headache.

Dead Sea Scrolls

Qumran, Jordan, 250 BC–AD 70

In 1947, two Bedouin shepherd boys found some jars in a cave at Khirbat Qumeran, north-west of the Dead Sea. Inside the jars were some leather scrolls with writing in Hebrew and Aramaic, two ancient languages of the Jews.

Archaeologists later investigated the caves and found more scrolls. Altogether there were 500 documents which seem to have formed the library of a Jewish community, called the Essene, who lived in the area over 2,000 years ago. The scrolls contain copies of all the Old Testament books of the Bible except Esther.

There are also commentaries, psalms and information about the community they belonged to. The scrolls are 1,000 years older than any copies of the Old Testament that have been found, and they are valuable examples of the ancient Hebrew and Aramaic scripts. The Essene may have hidden the scrolls away for safekeeping. Their settlement was destroyed by the Romans in AD 66–70.

▲ The Dead Sea Scrolls were stored in jars like this which helped them to survive for over 2,000 years.

The Dead Sea Scrolls had been written out by hand on long parchment rolls. Other copies of the Old Testament were made by Jewish scribes, but the scrolls did not survive long in the climate of Israel, so very few early or original documents have been found.

◀ This scroll of the Book of Isaiah dates from the 1st century AD, yet the leather is still intact and the writing clear.

Buried Cities

Pompeii & Herculaneum, Italy, AD 79

On 24 August in AD 79, Mount Vesuvius erupted and engulfed the Roman towns of Pompeii and Herculaneum in lava and volcanic ash. Thousands of people were killed, but the way in which the disaster happened meant that the towns were perfectly preserved.

When archaeologists discovered the towns again, they found intact houses with wall paintings and furnishings still in place and the bodies of people lying where they had fallen. They had choked on the volcanic gases as they tried to flee from the falling ash. The ash hardened round their bodies like a mould. When they were rediscovered, these 'moulds' were filled with plaster and dug out of the ash.

▲ This young woman died where she fell as she tried to flee from the ash and gases. Bodies were also found in cellars or bedrooms where the people had fled to protect themselves.

The Roman scholar, Pliny the Younger, was staying at a villa about 32 kilometres away when Vesuvius erupted. He wrote two letters about the eruption to the historian, Tacitus. His letters give interesting eyewitness details of the disaster.

Pompeii and Herculaneum were not large or important towns. We know that rich merchants lived well in villas with fine frescoes on the walls. The paintings show us that Roman ladies had slaves to do their housework. We can see details of clothes, hairstyles and furniture. There are shops with inscriptions on the walls, saying what they sold. These towns form a fascinating insight into Roman life.

◀ The walls of Pompeii with tombs beyond. Behind the town is Mount Vesuvius.

A Man in a Bog

Tollund Fen, Denmark, c. AD 100

In 1950, a group of peat-cutters found the body of an Iron Age man in the peat bog at Tollund Fen in Denmark. His face was perfectly preserved by the acid in the bog, and he looked as though he was sleeping peacefully. He had lain there undiscovered for about 2,000 years. Who was he and why was he buried in a bog? The strange thing is that, despite his peaceful expression, the man had a noose around his neck, showing that he had been hanged. Was he murdered or executed for a crime?

Tollund Man was not the first body to be discovered in the bog. Peat-cutters had found several bodies of Iron Age men and women over the years. Most of them had been strangled, hanged or had their throats cut. One young girl had been drowned. These earlier bodies were usually reburied without much

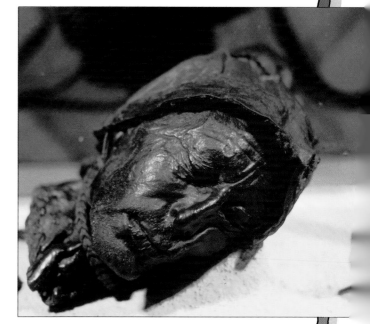

▲ Tollund Man wears a leather hat with a thong fastening. His hands showed no signs of manual labour, so he may have been a priest or a nobleman.

examination. But by the time Tollund Man was found, people realized the importance of such discoveries, and the finds were examined closely.

Tollund Man's stomach showed that he had eaten a meal of porridge not long before he died. The grains in the gruel were winter foods, so he must have died in winter. This discovery led to the belief that the bog people were not executed for crimes at all. Winters were long and hard in northern Europe, so rituals to make sure that spring arrived on time were almost certainly part of their religion.

The bog people could well have been sacrifices to ancient gods at the mid-winter celebrations. Another body, Grauballe Man, was found 17 kilometres from Tollund Man in 1952. His throat had been cut and his skull was fractured.

◄ The body has a noose round his neck, but his peaceful expression suggests that he did not struggle, so he may have been a willing sacrifice.

Hopewell Mound Burials

Ohio, USA, c. AD 100

The mound builders of North America fall into three groups. The earliest mounds were probably built by the Adena people from about 1000 BC. By about 300 BC, the Hopewell people had begun to build massive earthworks, which were used as burial places. The third group were the Mississippian people of Cahokia.

The Hopewell people buried their dead with much ceremony and many fine possessions. The grave goods found in Hopewell tell us a great deal about their craftwork. Burial mounds contain copper breastplates, ornate headdresses, finely sculptured figures and decorative pottery.

The interesting thing is that the materials from which these things were made came

▲ This pot is decorated with severed (cut off) hands and is connected with death rituals of the Hopewell people.

▶ This statue, made by Hopewell craftworkers, may have been of a shaman or medicine man. The knot on his forehead may represent the single horn, symbol of the shaman.

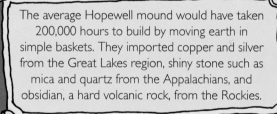

The average Hopewell mound would have taken 200,000 hours to build by moving earth in simple baskets. They imported copper and silver from the Great Lakes region, shiny stone such as mica and quartz from the Appalachians, and obsidian, a hard volcanic rock, from the Rockies.

from all over North America. Their raw materials were brought along narrow trails which connected villages all over North America. The Hopewell people were obviously skilful and creative but, despite their trading links, they did not try to dominate other tribes in North America. They traded by exchanging their craftwork for raw materials and lived peacefully in Ohio until the sixth century AD.

The Forts of Hadrian's Wall

England, c. AD 250

By the second century AD, the Romans controlled a massive empire which stretched from the Middle East and Egypt, right through Europe and into Britain. The empire enjoyed its most settled period at this time, under the rule of four great emperors. The second of these, Hadrian, who reigned from AD 117–38, brought Roman architecture to its peak.

The empire was always under threat from invaders, and Hadrian spent fifteen years travelling through its lands, ordering walls and ditches to be built as fortification. He came to Britain in AD 122 to find the Roman province of Britannia under attack from tribes from Scotland. Hadrian ordered a wall with forts for soldiers to be built to keep the invaders out.

▼ The idea of building a wall to keep out invaders may have been inspired by travellers' tales about the Great Wall of China.

▲ Objects such as Roman sandals like these have been found at Hadrian's Wall.

When the Romans took their soldiers out of England at the end of the fourth century, Picts and Scots poured across Hadrian's Wall to invade the south. There were later struggles between these invaders, the Romanized Britons and the Angles and Saxons who came from Germany and Denmark.

A General's Tomb

Shilla, South Korea, c. AD 250

Korea was once an isolated country made up of small farming communities. Ironworking was introduced into Korea in the fourth century BC, and the Han dynasty, the ruling family in China at about this time, ruled Korea from 108 BC. Both these developments brought more trading prospects and therefore greater wealth to Korea.

As Korea's prosperity grew, separate states began to form and develop into strongly organized communities. Ruling families began to emerge and a nobility developed. As a sign of their wealth and power, these people were buried in huge tombs which can still be seen today.

Wonderful grave goods have been found in the tombs at Shilla because they were hard to rob. A wooden construction containing the coffin was mounded with stones and earth.

▲ A crown made of silver and originally set with precious stones, found in a tomb at Shilla.

▼ The tomb of General Kim Yusin at Shilla. The large tomb is surrounded by pillars carved with signs of the zodiac and guardian figures to protect the dead.

The Chinese rulers introduced rice-growing to Korea and this took over from millet and soya beans as the staple food.

Silk Road Treasure

Begram, Afghanistan, c. AD 300

The Silk Road was an overland trade route which linked cities in the Near East to the Chinese cities of Chang'an and Luoyang. The goods carried by the merchants included silks, spices and bronze objects, all of which were very valuable. In return, merchants from the west sent ivory, coins and precious stones to the east.

The cities along the route became very wealthy by demanding a portion of the goods carried by the merchants. In return, the merchants were allowed to pass. Archaeologists have found many treasures which give us a very clear idea of trading at the time. One of the most famous finds was at the city of Begram in Afghanistan, which stood at the junction of three main trade routes. In 1938, Belgian archaeologists uncovered two storerooms which were filled with what came to be known as the Begram Treasure. There were ivory plaques and statues from India, bronze statues and glassware from Egypt, lacquerware from China and much more besides. The treasure had lain there, hidden away, for nearly 2,000 years.

▲ This magnificent ivory carving was found at Begram in Afghanistan. It probably shows a peri (Persian fairy) riding a griffin.

The Silk Road was 4,000 miles long. Marco Polo (c.1254–1324) travelled along it to Peking to meet the Mongol emperor Kublai Khan in 1271. Marco worked for Kublai Khan and sent accounts of his travels back to the West.

Yayoi People of Yoshinogari

Kyushu, Japan, c. AD 300

Yoshinogari was a settlement which was probably built in about 300 BC, when the Japanese began to develop their farming techniques. They learned how to grow rice in paddy-fields and to till the land more efficiently. The people became prosperous and by about AD 300, Yoshinogari was a large and thriving settlement. The time between 300 BC and 300 AD is known as the Yayoi period.

Yoshinogari may have been the centre of the Yayoi culture, but we do not know much about it. One mystery is the large burial mound which was found there. Nothing like it has been found anywhere else in Japan. It was obviously the tomb of someone important, but we do not know who.

Several thousand graves have also been found at Yoshinogari. The bodies

▲ An iron bell excavated at Yoshinogari. It may have been used in a temple.

had been buried in clay urns, and many of the skeletons show signs of terrible wounds. So the settlement was obviously the site of a bloody battle. But who it was against remains another of Yoshinogari's mysteries.

Chinese travellers to Japan in about 270–250 BC spoke of a place called Yamatai, which could be Yoshinogari. The Chinese travellers said that the ordinary people of Yamatai had to kneel when speaking to the nobles. If there was a strong ruling class, perhaps there was also a king or queen. That would explain the large burial mound.

Other finds at Yoshinogari tell us about everyday life. Archaeologists have found pottery and metalwork, which show that the Yayoi were skilled craftworkers.

Mithraeum

Rome, Italy & London, England, c. AD 370

A Mithraeum was a place where the Romans worshipped the god Mithras. He was a very popular god – a sun god and the god of love. The Romans also worshipped him for they believed he would bring victory in battle.

Mithraism began in ancient Persia (now Iran) in the fifteenth century BC, and spread to Europe about a hundred years before the birth of Christ. It soon had a strong following throughout the Roman empire. The religion expected loyalty, bravery and discipline, and so Roman emperors encouraged people to follow it because these qualities kept the Roman army under control.

We know very little about Mithraism because its rites and rituals were secret and mysterious, and most clues were lost when Mithraeums were destroyed by followers of Christianity. However, excavations have revealed a bit more.

▲ This carving shows the god, Mithras, slaying a bull. Mithraeans believed that corn and all other life came from the blood of the bull. Some historians believe that Mithraism was so popular that it would have become the main religion of the western world if Christianity had not taken over.

▼ The Mithraeum underneath the Church of St Clemente. This is one of 45 shrines dedicated to Mithras which have been found in Rome.

During the 1930s and 1950s, archaeologists excavated the ruins of a Mithraeum on Aventine Hill in Rome. It had been razed to the ground in about AD 400, and the Christians had built a church on the site.

Temple of the Sun

Teotihuacan, Mexico, AD 445

The city of Teotihuacan, about 50 km from Mexico City, was built about 200 BC. By AD 500, it was the sixth largest city in the world. But no one knows who built the city or who lived there.

The city was destroyed by fire in AD 750 and all of its people left. The Toltecs, and then the Aztecs, who both moved into this part of Mexico, found it ruined and deserted. The Aztecs probably copied its layout when they built their city of Tenochtitlan.

Archaeologists excavating Teotihuacan have found many temple goods among the ruins. In the centre of the city there was a wide roadway, the Avenue of the Dead. At one end stood a huge pyramid temple, the Pyramid of the Moon. About seventy-five smaller pyramids lined the avenue and to one side of it stood an even larger temple, the Pyramid of the Sun.

▲ This stone figure, with its oval eyes and mouth is a typical example of Teotihuacan sculpture from about AD 600.

▼ The Pyramids of the Sun and the Moon at Teotihuacan. The Pyramid of the Sun, the oldest and largest building in Teotihuacan, is 70 metres high.

The streets of Teotihuacan are laid out in a grid, which covers about 20 sq km. The Avenue of the Dead runs north to south and is over 5 km long. Carvings dedicated to Quetzalcoatl and Tlaloc, two gods also worshipped by the Aztecs, give us clues about the beliefs of the unknown people.

Tomb of the 15th Emperor

Mozu, Japan, c. AD 480

About 2,000 years ago, Japan was divided up into many separate states. One of these states was Yamato in south-east Japan. It was formed by ambitious rulers who wanted to gain power from the other states. The smaller states tried to resist, but the Yamato rulers were too strong and eventually all the states of Japan were united.

As Yamato society became more organized, the people began to construct large tombs or mound cemeteries to bury their dead. One of the most impressive of these is the cemetery at Mozu where Yamato's rulers are buried, surrounded by their nobles and courtiers.

The largest tomb of all is thought to belong to Nintoku, the fifteenth emperor, who ruled in the fifth century AD. The massive burial mound is 485 m long and shaped like a keyhole. It is so huge that no one is sure where the main burial chamber is.

However, in 1872 there was a landslide on the mound which revealed a secondary burial chamber near the bottom of the keyhole shape. Inside was a stone chest, or sarcophagus, where a body was laid surrounded with iron swords, a helmet and other objects for the afterlife.

Nintoku's burial mound was originally guarded by 23,000 pottery objects, or haniwa, which were supposed to protect the tomb.

▶ This terracotta 'haniwa' figure of a kneeling man was found at Yamato. It would have been placed on a burial mound to protect the dead person and the grave goods.

Kassapa's Palace-fortress

Sigiriya, Sri Lanka, AD 495

Buddhism was brought to Ceylon (now Sri Lanka) from India by a missionary in the third century BC. Buddhist monasteries began to appear all over the country. The rulers of Ceylon followed the new religion, but they also used it to promote themselves as godlike figures.

Shrines were set up as memorials to Buddha and also to the kings of Ceylon. Monasteries were often built at royal centres so that the kings could keep in contact with the monks. But not all Ceylonese royal architecture was religious. The palace-fortress at Sigiriya was built by Kassapa (AD 447–495) who had grasped power in Ceylon and believed that he was a god-king.

The palace was perched on top of a large rock and could only be reached by a walkway up the side of the rock. Once at the top, people were safe from attack as no one could approach without the greatest of difficulty.

▲ A statue of a dwarf from the rock fortress.

▼ The palace-fortress perched on a large rock with vertical sides. The main part of the palace was on the very summit of the rock, and the houses and other buildings which surrounded it were arranged at different levels. Visitors had to struggle up a walkway with a sheer drop to one side. Halfway up the rock were frescoes painted on boulders.

Buddhism is still the main religion in Sri Lanka today. It has dominated the country since its introduction in the third century BC. However, there is a large minority of Tamils in the north of the island who follow the Hindu religion. The civil war between the two groups is partly religious.

Potters of the Mochica

Viru Valley, Peru, c. AD 600

The Mochica people lived in the Viru Valley in Peru about 2,000 years ago. Today, the valley looks dry and lifeless, and it is hard to imagine how anyone lived there. But evidence uncovered by two American archaeologists in 1946 shows us that they did, and also that they had some strange customs.

When the two archaeologists excavated Viru, they found a grave containing five bodies. One of the bodies, a man, had been more important than the others – two women, a young man and a boy – who appear to have been buried alive to go with him to the afterlife.

The archaeologists found various grave goods with the bodies, including some strange clay pots. Each pot tells a

▲ This vessel shows a mountain sacrifice. At the foot of the seated figure (on the left) lies the victim, who has been thrown to his death from above. Other figures look on impassively.

▼ This pot shows a warrior wearing a helmet and carrying a shield. All the pots seem to have had a useful function as well as a decorative one.

The Mochica never invented a system of writing and, apart from their pots, they do not seem to have developed artistic skills. They don't seem to have had goldsmiths or jewellers as the Chima people to the south had.

different story. Some have a scene painted on them. Others are modelled to represent characters in a story. The scenes may be religious or show battles or aspects of everyday life, such as fishing, hunting and farming.

From these pots, archaeologists have been able to piece together evidence about the lives of the Mochica Indians from the first century BC until they disappeared around AD 700.

Basketmakers in the Drylands

Shabik'eschee, New Mexico, USA, c. AD 600

North American native peoples continued with a hunting and gathering lifestyle long after farming had been introduced to the continent, and both methods contributed equally to their diet. In the South-West, archaeologists have found the remains of wild foodstuffs and also the baskets used for collecting the food. These finds had been preserved because of the dry climate in that area.

Between AD 1 and 500, the Basketmakers, as these people are called, lived in small hamlets of up to eleven round houses. They grew maize as well as hunting and gathering. After AD 500, they moved to the river floodplains where they built larger villages like Shabik'eschee. These villages contained up to fifty houses.

A well-preserved house at Shabik'eschee consisted of one large rectangular room with a sunken floor, from which a corridor led to a circular antechamber. This had a conical roof with an opening which was the only door. The rectangular room had a flat roof with a hole for letting smoke out. There was a fire pit and another pit for grinding grain. The house was made of a pole and brush framework; the outer walls and roof were covered with earth and plaster.

▲ This black and white pitcher was made by people of the Anasazi culture in about AD 1000. The square design probably developed from the patterns made when weaving baskets.

◀ A basket made by the Salish, a tribe of North American Indians. Baskets like this would have been used for gathering plant food.

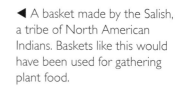

The people who lived in villages like Shabik'eschee hunted with bows and arrows. They also learned how to make pottery from the neighbouring Mogollon people.

Sutton Hoo Boat Burial

Suffolk, c. AD 630

In 1939, a treasure hoard was discovered at Sutton Hoo near Woodbridge in Suffolk. The treasure had been hidden inside a 24m ship and buried in a mound of earth. The find followed the Scandinavian method of burying people in ships to help them on their way to the afterlife.

Yet when the ship was excavated, no body was found in it. It was simply an elaborate memorial to an Anglo-Saxon king who had died in the seventh century and had been buried somewhere else. At that time, England was divided into small kingdoms, so he must have been a king of East Anglia, but no one knows his name. Probably he was a Christian and the boat memorial was to satisfy his pagan nobles that he would be suitably equipped for the afterlife.

▲ There was also this superb iron helmet decorated with gilding, silver and set with garnets.

The Angles and Saxons who came to England drove out much Roman culture, including the use of Latin, and introduced the first non-Mediterranean literature. The epic Anglo-Saxon poem *Beowulf* tells of events in fifth century Scandinavia when its hero, Beowulf, kills a terrible monster called Grendel who is terrorizing a nearby kingdom.

He was obviously very wealthy. Among the treasures was a magnificent, richly decorated belt buckle made of solid gold and weighing 412 g.

◀ Excavating the burial ship at Sutton Hoo. The treasure in it included a gold purse lid and two drinking horns.

Masters of the Calendar

Palenque & Copan, Central America, c. AD 700

The Mayan culture was one of the finest in Mexico and the Mayan civilization was one of the most important in Central American history. The Maya flourished on the Yucatan Peninsula between AD 300 and 900. Many of the people farmed the land, but the Maya built large ceremonial centres where the rulers, nobles and priests lived.

Palenque and Copan were two of these centres where important finds about the Mayan culture have been made. Each centre was dominated by pyramid temples and shrines, decorated with paintings and sculptures dedicated to the Mayan gods. Religion played an important part in the lives of the Maya,

▲ One side of the Mayan calendar stone from Copan. The figures carved on the stone are priests. The Maya believed that each day was controlled by a different god.

The Mayans were the first people in Central America to invent a system of writing using 'glyphs' where each picture symbol means a different word. They made many carvings and also books, three of which survive today.

and there is evidence that they made human sacrifices to the gods.

One of the most important contributions made by the Maya was the invention of a calendar which was carved in stone. Strangely, it began from the year 3113 BC. No one knows why. Dates were shown as the number of days that had passed since that year. The Maya broke time down into days, months and years, and believed that certain days were important for pleasing the gods.

◀ This tombstone comes from the heart of the great pyramid at Palenque. It covered the tomb of a Mayan king.

Treasures from the Silk Road

Shosoin Temple, Japan, AD 752

The temple of the Shosoin at Nara was built in AD 752 by the Emperor Shomu for the Dowager Empress. The emperor filled his new temple with treasures from all over Asia and Mediterranean lands. There were carpets from central Asia, lutes and masks from India, silver and bronze goods from Persia and glass from the eastern Mediterranean. There were numerous objects from China, including silk, lacquer, bronze and silver work. All these treasures had been carried along the Silk Road to Japan.

The Silk Road was an overland route for merchants to travel between the East and Europe. The cities along it became wealthy because they could control the trade and make the merchants pay for passing through. The cities became especially rich and powerful during the Tang dynasty in China (AD 618–907).

The Silk Road became less important during the Song dynasty (AD 960–1279) when safer and cheaper sea routes were opened up. There were many places where caravans could be attacked by bandits or marauding nomads along the route (see above).

◀ Goods have been carried along the Silk Road for thousands of years. There is evidence that Chinese silk appeared in the West as early as 550 BC. This Tang model of a camel with its driver shows the sort of people who actually travelled the Road.

Lombard Chief's Shield Boss

Stabio, Switzerland, c. AD 700

After the collapse of the Roman Empire at the end of the fourth century AD, there were many invasions into western Europe by the so-called barbarians. The most notorious, the Huns, came from the eastern plains of Europe. They were skilled horsemen and excellent archers, and they could invade an area very quickly. They galloped west, conquering everyone in their path.

Another tribe, the Visigoths, invaded the Balkans and Italy, and set up kingdoms in southern France and Spain. It was Alaric the Visigoth who sacked Rome in AD 410. The Vandals invaded Italy, too, before founding a kingdom in North Africa. The Franks also invaded Europe, and the Angles, Saxons and Jutes from northern Germany and Denmark settled in England.

The Lombards were one of the last tribes to sweep into Europe. They invaded modern Switzerland and northern and central Italy in about AD 600. However, their kingdom lasted for over 200 years. Their warrior culture was reflected in their art. This shield boss (decorative centrepiece) was found at Stabio in Switzerland.

When the barbarians settled in Europe, they built up a prosperous culture. Many of them were skilled craftworkers in gold and other precious metals.

▼ A mounted warrior, which was part of a Lombard chief's shield, shows the rider galloping into battle. He carries a lance, which is drawn back ready to strike at the enemy. He is made of bronze.

Sailing to Heaven

Oseberg, Norway, c. AD 820

The Vikings were seafarers who made many voyages of exploration in the eighth and ninth centuries. So it is not surprising that ships were an important part of their burial traditions. They believed that when a person died, the spirit sailed off to an afterlife. Royalty and wealthy nobles were often buried in a ship together with food and possessions for the journey.

Much of our knowledge about Viking ships comes from excavations of burial ships in Norway. The Oseberg ship was excavated in 1903. It had been buried in clay, so the wood had not rotted, and so it was almost complete. The ship held the body of a noblewoman. Horses, an ox, a sledge, a cart and a tent were buried with her. The ship was about 21.5 m long by 5 m wide and beautifully decorated.

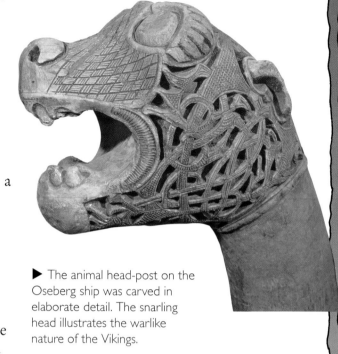

▶ The animal head-post on the Oseberg ship was carved in elaborate detail. The snarling head illustrates the warlike nature of the Vikings.

The Vikings worshipped pagan gods, such as Odin and Thor. Ship burials were no longer carried out after they were converted to Christianity. Less wealthy people did not have such elaborate burials. They were cremated or buried in an ordinary grave and the place was marked with stones in the shape of a boat.

Burial of a Prince

Igbo Ukwu, Nigeria, c. AD 850

Igbo Ukwu was the centre of a small kingdom near the edges of the tropical forests. A tomb was found there, and in it was a man buried sitting upright in a wooden chamber pit. On his head he wore a bead headdress and a copper crown. He also wore a breastplate, anklets and strings of beads, and he was holding a fly whisk.

These items show he was a member of the royal family or a noble who had lived around AD 850. The tomb contained other items, such as a copper plate and ivory tusks, which may have been possessions for the afterlife. The bodies of five people, probably slaves, had been placed on top of the chamber.

These finds tell us about an interesting time in West Africa, when the first kingdoms were developing and royal families and nobility were establishing

▲ This ornate bronze head-dress was cast by the 'lost wax' method. Very intricate designs can be introduced using this technique.

Ancestor worship was an important part of African religion. Many shrines contained small statues of human figures which may have represented ancestors.

themselves. The kingdoms were established as local people banded together to control trade in wood from the forests. This allowed them to become involved in trading over a large part of Africa. Copper and salt were mined in the Sahara, while the savannah regions traded gold. The rulers of small kingdoms such as Igbo Ukwu grew rich as trading increased.

◄ These Igbo cult figures were connected with food-growing rituals.

Viking Warrior's Tomb

Fittja, Sweden, c. AD 950

The Vikings were known as raiders and traders, and they certainly did both. They would set off on raiding trips in their longships, terrorizing the people of the countries they invaded.

The *Anglo Saxon Chronicle* records a raid in AD 787 when three boatloads of Vikings raided Dorset in England. Six years later, they raided the monastery at Lindisfarne off the coast of Scotland where they 'laid everything to waste with grievous plundering, trampled the holy places with dirty feet, dug up the altars and seized all the treasures of the holy church'.

But by the tenth century, the raiding was almost over and the Vikings began a more peaceful lifestyle. Instead of plundering, they set up trading links all over Europe. They built special cargo ships and travelled along rivers as well as across the sea.

The grave of a trader in Sweden shows us how far Vikings travelled. The trader had been buried with his wealth for his journey to the afterlife. When archaeologists opened the grave, they found silver pieces from Spain, Egypt, Syria, Baghdad and from the city of Tashkent in Central Asia.

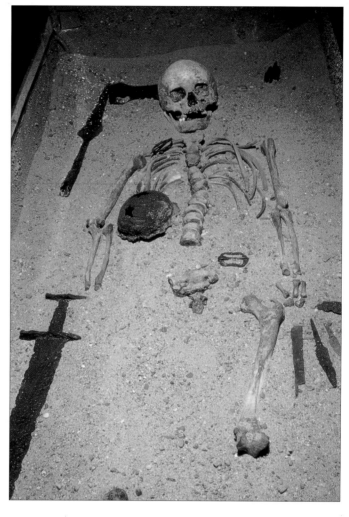

▲ This Viking died when raiding was still the main way of life. He was buried with his axe, spear and sword by his side. He also has knives, a shield and a belt buckle.

When the Vikings had to travel overland, they lifted their boats out of the water and carried them or rolled them on logs. In winter they skated from place to place on frozen rivers and lakes.

Cities in the Canyons

Pueblo Bonito, Chaco Canyon, USA, AD 950–1300

Civilizations did not develop in North America in the same way that they did elsewhere. The North American Indians lived in separate communities, each one with its own culture and lifestyle. By AD 700, there were three main cultures in the South-West of North America. They were the Hohokam, the Mogollon and the Anasazi peoples.

The largest of these groups was the Anasazi, who lived in an area known as the Four Corners, where the boundaries of New Mexico, Colorado, Utah and Arizona meet. This is a region of high plateaux and deep canyons.

In one, the huge Chaco Canyon, the Anasazi built a town called Pueblo Bonito where about 1,200 people lived. It was surrounded by a protective outer wall in the shape of a 'D'. Inside the wall were over 800 rooms where the people lived. There were twelve other towns in the canyon and about 400 km of roads linking them.

Each town had its kiva or ceremonial room where the people could meet to discuss the planting of crops, plan rituals and deal with the running of the community. It was also the religious centre of the town. The towns of Chaco Canyon were abandoned soon after AD 1300, perhaps because the crops failed and the people had to move on, or because of attacks from other tribes. But the evidence the Anasazi left behind about their lives continues to fascinate archaeologists and visitors to the area.

▼ The sides of the canyon offered some protection to the people of Pueblo Bonito, but the D-shaped outer wall was still needed to keep out invaders.

The Anasazi feared attack from other tribes and so they fortified their towns or built them in inaccessible places, like the settlements high in the canyon cliffs at Mesa Verde.

Beating Columbus

Newfoundland, Canada, c. AD 1000

Evidence from Newfoundland, off the coast of Canada, shows that the Vikings reached North America nearly 1,000 years ago, long before Columbus sailed to the West Indies in 1492.

About AD 985, a Viking named Bjarni Herjolfsson was blown off course on an expedition and saw the coast of North America. He did not land, but returned to the Viking colony on Greenland to spread the news about this strange new land.

Leif Erikson set sail to find this new land, which he named Vinland. It seems Erikson tried to settle in Newfoundland, but the Vikings do not seem to have stayed in their new land for long. Perhaps it was too far from home or there were too few people to make the settlement work.

▼ This modern reconstruction of a Viking ship shows how hardy Leif and his men must have been.

During the 1960s, archaeologists found the foundations of a Viking house and the site of a smithy at L'Anse aux Meadows. This is thought to have been the first Viking settlement in North America.

Caves of the Thousand Buddhas

Dunhuang, China, c. AD 1020

For hundreds of years, Buddhist monks made pilgrimages to remote cave temples in Dunhuang on the edge of the Gobi Desert in western China. Dunhuang had been a stopping place on the Silk Road, but when the route was abandoned, the town was forgotten. Over the years, the cave temples fell into disrepair.

At the end of the nineteenth century, a Buddhist monk named Wang Tao-Shah organized a group of workmen to clear out the Magoa caves, now choked with desert sand. As they dug, one workman found a secret chamber containing thousands of ancient manuscripts and other treasures. Wang reported his discovery, but was told to seal up the caves again and stand guard over them.

The British archaeologist Aurel Stein heard rumours about the incredible find and wanted to stake a claim in it. Stein

The manuscripts and other treasures in the caves may have been hidden away from Mongol horsemen who conquered Dunhuang in the eleventh century. Visitors to the caves themselves can see the 1,000 Buddhist sculptures which give the caves their name. The walls are decorated with paintings which give a fascinating view of life in ancient China.

and his team persuaded the monk to let them see some of the manuscripts and gradually removed many of them from the caves. Today, about 3,000 manuscripts as well as textiles and paintings from the caves are in the British Museum in London.

◀ There are many Buddhist monuments in the area around the Magoa Caves. The landscape is wild and desolate.

Largest Town in America

Cahokia, Illinois, USA, 1100–1300

In the Mississippi Valley, Native Americans built towns on mounds which lifted the towns above the flat floodplain. Rectangular plazas separated the mounds. Cahokia was the central town for nine large settlements, each one with its one chief, and numerous smaller hamlets and farms.

Cahokia was the largest town and ceremonial centre built in North America before the days of the European settlers. Today, its remains lie under the town of Saint Louis, Missouri. The town was built on more than a hundred flat-topped mounds. The largest of these, Monk's Mound, was 30 m high and covered 6.5 hectares. The remains of a temple was found there, which stood at the centre of the mound and was a focal point for the whole community. Other mounds were burial places.

In about 1200, the central part of the town was enclosed by a wooden stockade, presumably as protection against invasion. Cahokia's chiefs lived within this central complex which contained Monk's Mound, smaller temple mounds, a great plaza and burial mounds for important people.

▲ This axe has been carved from one piece of slate. Several have been found; they were probably used in ceremonies.

▼ Mound A at Etowah near Cartersville in Georgia. This mound was built gradually over many years, not in one big operation.

In one burial mound, the body of a chief lay on a platform of 20,000 shell beads. Three other people had been buried nearby. They may have been relatives who were sacrificed at the chief's funeral. Near them lay a variety of grave goods including about 800 arrowheads.

Moa-hunters' Camp

Wairau Bar, New Zealand, c. 1150

The first people to settle in New Zealand, the Maori, arrived there in about AD 1000. They found the cool climate of New Zealand very different to what they were used to – they had come from the warm, tropical Polynesian islands of the Pacific Ocean.

The settlers may have tried to introduce many different tropical plants which they had brought with them, but these would not flourish on the South Island of New Zealand, where the weather was too cold. On the North Island, they did manage to grow some traditional crops, particularly the sweet potato.

So these settlers had to find some other form of food in order to survive. They became hunters and gatherers, relying on supplies of animals, fish, birds and local plants. As no one had ever lived on the islands before, there was plenty of natural food to be had, including a very large flightless bird called the moa, a relative of the ostrich.

A moa-hunters' camp and cemetery discovered at Wairau Bar has one of the finest collection of grave goods ever found in New Zealand – most of these have connections with the moa. The hunters and their families were buried with necklaces made of moa bones, specially decorated moa eggs and other ornaments. Not far from the burial ground was a campsite, where more moa bones were found.

However, the moa was too easy a target for the hunters, and it became extinct by about 1500. By then, however, people had learned how to farm the land, and agriculture became the most important source of food.

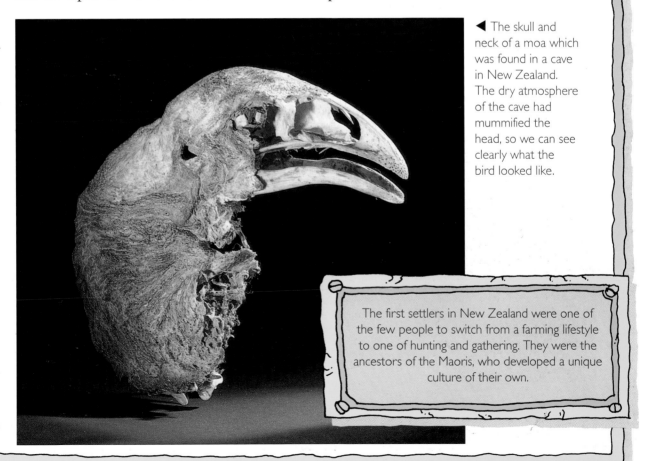

◀ The skull and neck of a moa which was found in a cave in New Zealand. The dry atmosphere of the cave had mummified the head, so we can see clearly what the bird looked like.

The first settlers in New Zealand were one of the few people to switch from a farming lifestyle to one of hunting and gathering. They were the ancestors of the Maoris, who developed a unique culture of their own.

Temple of the Warriors

Chichen Itza, Mexico, c. 1150

During the tenth century, various nations invaded Mexico and tried to settle there. The most successful were the Toltecs, a warlike people who conquered other cities and took food from them to support their army.

However, the Toltecs were also skilled builders and sculptors. Their ceremonial centre at Chichen Itza was dedicated to Quetzalcoatl, the Feathered or Plumed Serpent god, and contains many interesting artefacts. Chichen Itza was originally built by the Maya, who lived in the Yucatan Peninsula between AD 300 and 900. After their civilization collapsed, the Toltecs built a new ceremonial centre to the north of the Mayan city in about 1100.

The Toltecs believed that Quetzalcoatl would postpone the end of the world if they kept him happy with offerings of human blood and hearts. But the god was unkind and the Toltecs' domination of Mexico ended in about 1170, paving the way for the Aztecs.

▲ Dominating Chichen Itza was the stepped pyramid, which stood in the centre of the town. The Temple of the Warriors (foreground) stood to the west. Its entrance was guarded by a reclining figure and two open-jawed feathered serpents.

▼ These fierce warriors used to hold up the roof of the pyramid temple in the Toltec capital at Tula.

A Lost City

Great Zimbabwe, Zimbabwe, c. 1200

In 1871, a German geologist, Karl Mauch, discovered the ruins of a stone city deep in the bush country of southern Africa. This surprised him greatly since the traditional building materials in Africa were wood and mud. The people living in the area called the ruins Zimbabwe ('stone houses').

The main building is a large enclosure which stands on a hilltop, dominating the town. It may have been the palace of the chief and his family. In the valley below there is a temple inside a walled enclosure. Houses are scattered between the two. Most of the town dates back to about 1200, when the Mbire people were in control of the area.

▼ The ruins of Great Zimbabwe. The Conical Tower is 10.4 metres high. It may have been used for ritual ceremonies or it could have represented the power of a chief.

The Mbire were excellent craftworkers and skilled miners. They were also traders who provided raw materials in exchange for luxury foreign goods. So they probably built most of the stone city. But why did they build it in stone instead of more traditional materials? Perhaps because it was a religious centre, but more probably to reflect its importance as a trading city.

The inhabitants of Great Zimbabwe finally deserted it in the sixteenth century – probably because the food and timber supplies had run out.

Archaeologists have found luxury foreign goods in the ruins, including Chinese and Islamic pottery and shells and beads from coastal areas. So Great Zimbabwe was probably built as a trading centre.

Moundville Burials

Alabama, USA, c. 1250

Moundville was built by the Mississippian people on the banks of the Black Warrior River in Alabama. By the thirteenth century, it was a major religious centre where about 3,000 people lived. It consisted of twenty large platform mounds built round a large rectangular plaza.

The largest mound was 18 m high and covered about 1 hectare in area. The central part of the town was surrounded by a protective wall on three sides. The fourth side was open to the river.

Archaeologists have deduced a lot of information about the people who lived at Moundville from about 3,000 burials which have been examined there. There was a ruling class who had probably been born into the nobility. These people lived in large houses on the platform mounds. When they died they were buried in or near the mounds with a selection of lavish grave goods including ceremonial axes, masks and shell ornaments. The chief was buried in a large mound together with sacrificial victims.

The rest of the people lived outside the town, and were buried more simply. Some had no grave goods at all. Only adult males had ceremonial axes, and children always had fewer goods than adults. They were not buried in or near the mounds.

The people of Moundville lived by farming and fishing. They also took gifts from less powerful people in neighbouring settlements. This system is known as tribute and was a feature of many Native American cultures like the Maya and the Incas.

▼ Shell discs like this one were often worn as chest decoration by followers of a Mississippian religion known as the Southern Cult. This one shows a spider. The cross in the middle is a symbol of the sacred fire.

55034

Artists in Gold

Chan-Chan, Peru, c. 1400

The Chima civilization built up an empire which dominated northern Peru from about AD 700 until they were defeated by the Incas in 1476. Their capital city was Chan-Chan, which covered more than 15 sq km. At the centre of the city were ten royal compounds, which were built over a period of 250 years. But why ten compounds?

Each compound must have belonged to a Chima king. When a king died, his compound was sealed up and became his tomb, and a new compound was built for the next king. Each compound contained a huge entrance courtyard with the royal apartments and a maze of storerooms and small courtyards behind it. The king's burial platform lay in readiness, surrounded by rooms containing treasures for the king to take to the afterlife.

The Chima were skilled goldsmiths, and archaeologists have found many examples of their work at Chan-Chan. The gold was exquisitely worked, and was covered with detailed designs. The Incas, famous for their hoards of gold, copied Chima techniques after they had conquered them.

The Chima kings were probably treated

▲ The gold necklace and llama ornament were made by the Incas following techniques they had learned from the Chima.

The Chima had no money and so they used woven fabrics as payment for tax and tribute. Remains of textiles were found in what must have been the royal treasury.

like gods, as the Inca rulers were. Perhaps they took the gold with them to the afterlife to ensure that they were treated with respect there. They also executed hundreds of women to accompany the king on his journey.

◄ This gold duck vase shows the realistic style of Chima workmanship.

A Tudor Wreck

The Solent, England, 1545

The *Mary Rose* was built in 1509 at Portsmouth in England. Henry VIII had become king of England that year, and was keen to build up a strong fleet. She was a successful ship, able to carry heavy guns without becoming unstable, and was used against France in 1513.

Unfortunately, in 1545, the *Mary Rose* sank during a battle with the French. She was about 2 km from Portsmouth Harbour in about 14 m of water. Very few of the crew survived and the ship was not seen again for over 400 years.

In 1965, a team of divers began to search for the wreck on the sea-bed. When she was eventually found, divers, scientists and archaeologists began the underwater excavation. By 1982, the whole ship had been excavated and, on 11 October, she was raised from the sea-bed. She can now be seen in Portsmouth.

▲ Sailors would have kept themselves occupied during a voyage by playing board games such as this one, found on the *Mary Rose*.

▼ The *Mary Rose* was a strong, heavy ship which could tackle rough seas and carry large guns without becoming unbalanced.

In 1513, Sir Edward Howard used the *Mary Rose* as a flagship in the war with France, and wrote to the King about 'your good ship, the flower I trow of all ships that ever sailed'.

Landslide at Ozette

Washington, USA, c. 1550

Ozette is a small village on the north-western coast of Washington state. For 2,000 years, it was the home of the Makah Native Americans, who only moved to a nearby town in the 1930s. The Makah were whale hunters who chased them in their dug-out canoes. All their old settlements had disappeared – until 1970, when a stormy sea caused a landslip, which revealed a wooden longhouse. It had been buried under a 2m thick layer of mud which had preserved it perfectly.

The Makah had no written records which were older than 100 years, but stories had been handed down through the generations. One told of a massive avalanche of mud which had buried the houses and their inhabitants. This longhouse had been buried in that disaster, dated to the fifteenth century. It was a large house divided into separate units, each with its own cooking hearth and sleeping platforms. This meant that several families had lived there. The families' belongings were still lying around inside, as they had been when disaster struck.

▼ Ozette from the air. To the left is the spit of sand which joins up with Cannonball Island at low tide. The Makah hid on the island when threatened.

The Makah people sometimes cooked by putting red-hot stones into wooden boxes filled with water.
Owls were a part of Makah rituals so this club with an owl head (shown above) may have been carried by a shaman.

Towering Temples

Vijayanagara, India, 1565

Before the fourteenth century, southern India had been divided between the empires of the Pallava, the Pandya, the Chola and the Hoysala dynasties. The ruling families were rivals for power and each had periods when they were dominant over the others.

Vijayanagara became the dominant state in the middle of the fourteenth century (which is when the capital city was founded), and remained so until it was destroyed by Muslim invaders in 1565. The royal city of Vijayanagara was the capital of this kingdom which lay in the Krishna Valley. It was one of the most magnificent capital cities in Asia, with its stunning temples to Hindu gods and goddesses.

The city was abandoned in 1565 and so became ruined. These ruins, which cover an area of 25 sq km, can still be seen today. There is the royal palace, a temple complex with temples to

▲ The ruins of Vijayanagara include massive fortified walls surrounding religious and residential areas. The sacred centre of the city, with its temples, is to the north of the palace.

different Hindu gods, and an impressive elephant stable, all reminders of this once-powerful temple city.

▼ A carving of one of the great Hindu gods, Vishnu.

The Cholas dominated southern India from the ninth to the twelfth centuries, and built many temples where their kings were worshipped as gods. The pyramid-shaped Brihadishvara temple at Thanjavur is an outstanding example of their architecture.

The Wreck of the *Amsterdam*

Hastings, England, 1749

On 26 January 1749, a ship from the Dutch East India Company ran aground near Hastings, on the south coast of England. There were 300 people on board. The *Amsterdam* was on her maiden voyage from the Netherlands to Java in Indonesia, carrying a large mixed cargo which included cloth, wines and silver. Bullion (solid gold and silver) was in great demand by merchants in the Far East.

The voyage was ill-fated from the start. Disease had broken out on board and fifty men had died. Forty others were very sick. The crew was already rebellious when the ship ran into strong gales and lost her rudder. So the crew mutinied and insisted that the captain run her ashore as soon as possible. Disaster struck when the *Amsterdam* hit the soft clay of the sea-bed. She sank so quickly that nothing could be saved from her except the silver.

▲ When the wreck was excavated, most of the cargo was still on board and the ship was almost complete. She is the best surviving example of an eighteenth-century European ship in the world.

▼ Some of the fascinating, everyday objects found in the *Amsterdam* during her excavation.

The Dutch East India Company was formed by a group of merchants to trade between the Netherlands and India, China, Japan and the East Indies. Ships plied back and forth, carrying cargoes of lead, copper, wines and other goods from Europe and returning with silks, spices, furniture and porcelain from the East.

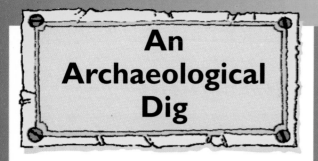

An Archaeological Dig

Part I

Use the clues to fill in the missing initial letters of the words below. The initial letters, when read downwards, form other words. If you are stuck, you will find the answer on the page given in [ ].

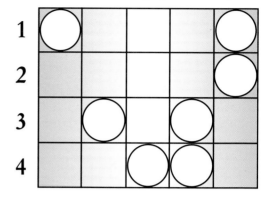

Part 2

Write the words you have found going down the page in this grid:

If you then take the circled letters and rearrange them, you can find the name of the place (two words) where scrolls of the Old Testament were found.

Homo ------- is our first true ancestor [13]	**1** _ APIENS
One of the towns buried by Mt Vesuvius [75]	_ OMPEII
Ancient language of the Jews [74]	_ RAMAIC
Country where the Bog Man was found [76]	_ ENMARK
City of ancient Syria [32]	_ BLA

Collection of clay tablets found at Ebla -[32]	**3** _ IBRARY
Very old, antique [57]	_ NCIENT
Land where the Mayan people flourished [89]	_ UCATAN
The homeland of the Etruscans [61]	_ TRURIA
Pharaoh who advertised his victories [28]	_ AMESES

_ INERAL	**2** Ochre is one, used for paint in cave art [22]
_ LDUVAI	The gorge where bones of *Homo habilis* were found [11]
_ KRAINE	The mammoth hut is in this country [20]
_ INEVEH	A city built by the Assyrians [48]
_ WARF	A statue of one was found at Sigiriya [85]

_ ABYLON	**4** Where Hammurabi drew up his laws [39]
_ ACQUER	Material used to decorate wood [58]
_ LABAMA	The Moundville burials are in this US state [102]
_ AGGER	Many warriors were buried with one [51]
_ XTINCT	Having died out [20]

GALWAY COUNTY LIBRARIES

Answers can be found on page 111

108

Index

Picture Acknowledgements

a = above, b = below

AKG, London: 90b. Ancient Art and Architecture Collection: 12a, 12b, 18b, 28a, 29a, 32a, 32b, 36, 39a, 40, 41, 42, 45b, 50, 57, 60a, 60b, 61b, 62a, 62b, 63, 66b, 68a, 68b, 69a, 69b, 70a, 72, 74a, 74b, 75a, 76a, 78a, 83a, 86b, 88a, 89a, 93b, 95, 96, 97b, 100b, 103b. Ardea: 14. Bridgeman Art Library: 104b (Private Collection). British Museum: 88b, 97a. C.M. Dixon: 8a, 8b, 9b, 13, 17a, 18a, 19, 20, 22, 29b, 30a, 31b, 33a, 33b, 34a, 34b, 35b, 37b, 39b, 43a, 44a, 49a, 51a, 51b, 54a, 54b, 55a, 55b, 61a, 64a, 64b, 65, 66a, 73, 78b, 85a, 85b, 86a, 87b, 92a, 94. Mary Evans Picture Library: 70b. Werner Forman

Archive: 23 (Maxwell Museum of Anthropology, Albuquerque), 31a, 35a (Edgar Knobloch), 47 (Anthropology Museum, Veracruz), 59 (National Museum, Lagos), 75b, 77a (Smithsonian Institute, Washington), 77b (Peabody Museum, Harvard University), 79a (San Francisco Museum of Asiatic Art), 79b, 80b, 82a (Museo Nazionale Romano, Rome), 82b, 83b, 84 (Ono Collection, Osaka), 87a (Maxwell Museum of Anthropology, Albuquerque), 92b (Viking Ship Museum, Bygdoy), 93a (National Museum, Lagos), 99 (National Museum of New Zealand), 100a, 101, 102 (Field Museum of Natural History, Chicago). Sonia Halliday: 43b (F.H.C. Birch). Robert Harding: 10a, 24a, 24b, 30b, 45a, 46a, 46b, 71a (G. & P. Corrigan), 71b, 103a, 104a, 106a, 106b, 107a, 107b

(Adam Woolfitt). Historical Museum, Bern: 91. Hulton-Deutsch Collection: 56a. Illustrated London News Picture Library: 15a, 15b, 25, 26b, 44b, 48, 76b. Image Select: 90a. National Museum of Afghanistan, Kabul: 80a. National Museum of Japan, Tokyo: 81. Natural History Museum Picture Library: 9a, 10b, 11a, 11b. Novosti: 16. Ann and Bury Peerless: 67a. Pictures of Record: 98a, 98b, 105a, 105b. Pre-Columbian Art Research Institute, California: 89b (Merle Greene Robertson). Graeme Pretty, University of Adelaide: 27. Scala: 26a. Frank Spooner: 38a & 38b (Gamma).

Paintings on page 36, 52, 67, 81 and 84 reproduced by kind permission of Robert Ingpen. Maps by Keith Madison

COVER CREDITS
front, clockwise from top left:

Ancient Art and Architecture Collection, C.M. Dixon, Ancient Art & Architecture Collection, Werner Forman Archive (National Museum of New Zealand), Ancient Art & Architecture Collection and following three, Werner Forman Archive (Anthropology Museum, Veracruz), Robert Harding, Ancient Art & Architecture Collection, Ancient Art & Architecture Collection. Back, clockwise from top left: Natural History Museum Picture Library, Werner Forman Archive (Viking Ship Museum, Bygdoy), Werner Forman Archive, Ancient Art & Architecture Collection, Ancient Art & Architecture Collection, Werner Forman Archive (Ono Collection), C.M. Dixon, Ancient Art & Architecture Collection, Ancient Art & Architecture Collection, Sonia Halliday.